LORD, TEACH ME TO PRAY
IN 28 DAYS

KAY ARTHUR

HARVEST HOUSE PUBLISHERS
Eugene, Oregon 97402

Cover by Left Coast Design, Portland, Oregon.

Lord, Teach Me to Pray in 28 Days
Copyright © 1982, 1955 by Kay Arthur
Published by Harvest House Publishers
Eugene, Oregon 97402

Library of Congress Cataloging-in-Publication Data
  p. cm.
  ISBN 1-56507-252-9
  1. pRAYER. I. Title.
BV215.A77 1994   94-29310
248.8382—dc20   CIP

00 01 02 03 04 / BP / 14 13

Contents

Where we should be the strongest, we're the weakest. Is this why so many who profess Christ live such impotent and ordinary lives? Why so many people, even those who have been "well-known" in the Western world of Christianity, have "fallen into sin"?

When the apostles of the early church suddenly found themselves embroiled in a controversy that consumed both their time and energy, they had enough spiritual presence of mind to know that something had to be done. They were in danger of missing the priority of their calling—the Word of God and prayer! Thus they summoned "the congregation of the disciples and said, 'It is not desirable for us to neglect the word of God in order to serve tables. But select from among you, brethren, seven men of good reputation, full of the Spirit and of wisdom, whom we may put in charge of this task. But we will devote ourselves to prayer, and to the ministry of the word'" (Acts 6:2–4).

This is where each child of God should be the strongest: in the Word of God and in prayer. Why the Word of God? Because according to Jesus, man lives by every word which comes out of the mouth of God, and that's what the Word of God is (Matthew 4:4). It is God-breathed. The word *inspiration* in 2 Timothy 3:16 comes from the Greek word *thĕŏpnĕustŏs* which means "God-breathed." This is why both my life and Precept Ministries are devoted to teaching people how to study God's Word for themselves. We exist in order to establish God's people in His Word as that which produces a life lived in reverence toward God.

My, how Christendom in general lacks a fear—a reverence—of God! That's why there is so much sin, so much self-centered living and so little embracing of the Cross.

The Word of God is the foundation for everything else in our lives. When God speaks on any given issue, what He speaks is truth. What He commands is to be obeyed. God has spoken, and it stands. We are to believe and obey.

Yet Christianity is more than merely believing and obeying commands and promises. Christianity is not a religion; it is a relationship. And a relationship requires communication. Therefore, prayer is essential, because it is through prayer that you and I communicate with our heavenly Father. There are countless decisions to be made, wisdom to be sought, resources that are needed, transgressions to be mended, love and appreciation to be communicated. Thus, we are told to pray without ceasing. The aspects of our daily living may be found in the Word of God in principle but not necessarily in practical detail. Therefore, we need to talk with and listen to our heavenly Father. This is prayer.

The disciples had to be careful, lest they become so occupied with serving God that they neglect the Word, which is knowing God, and prayer, which is communicating with Him.

When Jesus was with the disciples on earth, they saw the place of prayer in His life and they heard His teaching on the importance of persistence in prayer. Thus, realizing that they had to know how to pray, they said, "Lord, teach us to pray."

If they needed to know, don't we? Of course! As a matter of fact, Beloved, the more you give yourself to prayer and the Word of God, the stronger will be the one relationship that is to have preeminence over everything else.

So here it is: not another book on prayer, but a study of Jesus' response to His disciples when they said, "Lord, teach us to pray," and He said, "When you pray, say . . . ."

The study you are about to do has already been done by over 450,000 people, and the reports of its success have been more than encouraging. They've been exciting. And that is only to be expected, because what you are going to do is simply dig into the Word of God for yourself and learn in greater depth the Lord's way to pray.

Your study will take only four weeks—just twenty-eight days. However, what you learn will be yours to put into practice for a lifetime.

As you work through this study or after you complete it, you may want to read other books on prayer. Certainly there's no lack of books on the subject. Some are absolute treasures. However, there are others that do not have a solid biblical basis, so you need to choose with discernment. Besides, do we really need to go beyond the Scriptures and what they teach about prayer? I think not, but I will leave that for you to decide.

This study book is offered with the prayer that God will use it mightily to teach you to pray "according to His will" and that His words on prayer will abide in you. Remember, Jesus said, "If you abide in Me, and My words abide in you, ask whatever you wish, and it shall be done for you" (John 15:7).

You can use this book for group studies, prayer groups, Sunday school classes, discipleship material, or simply on your own—alone. Whichever you choose, just use it and see what happens when you put it into practice.

If you would like audio or video teaching tapes to accompany this study book, or leader's tapes to assist you in leading a class in this study, let us know. Simply contact our Customer Services Department, Precept Ministries, P.O. Box 182218, Chattanooga, Tennessee, 37422 (423-892-6814).

We were having a prayer time at one of our women's conferences at Precept Ministries when one of the women asked us to pray for a member of her church who was lying in a hospital, riddled with cancer and at the brink of death.

"Would you please pray for healing?" the woman said.

Debra Martin, one of our staff at the time, was manning the roving microphone, so I asked her to pray. Debra's prayer came slowly, with hesitation. I could tell that she was struggling with a question—a question that was in my heart as well: "How do I pray, Lord?"

Now I can just hear some of the "brethren" or "sistern" say, "Struggle! Why struggle? Where's her faith? Doesn't she believe God can heal? Doesn't she know the promises? Doesn't Scripture say if we ask anything in His name that He'll do it? What about the verse that says 'according to your faith be it unto you'?"

Yes, Debra knew the promises, and she knew that God can and does heal. The problem was that she did not know God's will for this particular person.

"God's will! God's will!" Again I can hear some of you. "God's will is to heal! Healing is for everyone if we just have the faith to claim it!"

If you are nodding your head in assent to that last statement, I know where you are coming from, and we will cover it later in our study. However, right now

I don't want to get off track, because we have just one objective: "Lord, teach me to pray."

Have you ever been put in a situation like Debra's? If people know you believe in prayer, I am sure you have. What did you do? How did you pray? Did God answer your prayer? Did you know for sure that He would? Or, if He did, were you surprised?

Let me ask you a few more questions while I'm at it. How confident are you in your prayer life? Have you ever believed God would answer your prayer a certain way, only to be disappointed? When you pray, are your prayers general prayers like, "Bless everyone. Help all the missionaries. Heal all the sick"? Are you afraid to pray specifically, to ask God for definite answers?

Oh, Beloved, believe me I do understand. I've been there. And since I have been there, do you mind if I ask a few more questions?

Do you ever stand in absolute awe at the testimony of others and their answers to prayer? Does it make you feel like a reject because you have never received those kinds of answers? Does it make you jealous . . . envious . . . or downright mad? Do you ever wonder if you even know how to pray? Or have you even wondered if God really meant what He said when He gave us some of those prayer promises? Are you frustrated in your prayer life? Do you read books on prayer, get all excited or convicted, start out with a bang, and then fizzle out?

Bless your heart. Let me say again that I understand. And although I do not claim to be a pro when it comes to prayer, I can share with you the principles from God's Word that we all need to know in order to pray effectively, in order to get our prayers answered. These are basic. They're simple. They're biblical. Thus, they work! All you need is practice.

Willing? Good! Now determine before God that you are going to finish what you start. In other words, determine that you are going to spend the next twenty-eight days sitting at His feet, learning what He means when He says, "Pray, then, in this way . . ." (Matthew 6:9).

Today, your assignment is to read the following verses from 1 John. After you have read them, I will tell you what to do.

"And this is the confidence which we have before Him, that, if we ask anything according to His will, He hears us. And if we know that He hears us in whatever we ask, we know that we have the requests which we have asked from Him" (1 John 5:14–15).

According to these verses, if you ask anything that is God's will, you can know that He will hear and answer your prayer.

Is it God's will for you to know how to pray?

Then go to God in prayer, tell Him what you want regarding prayer, show Him His promise, and claim it.

Write out your prayer. Keep it simple, short, and to the point. God doesn't hear better just because we pray longer!

Notes

You have often heard, "The effectual fervent prayer of a righteous man availeth much" (James 5:16 KJV). Yet what does it mean?

James goes on to say, "Elijah was a man with a nature like ours, and he prayed earnestly that it might not rain; and it did not rain on the earth for three years and six months. And he prayed again, and the sky poured rain, and the earth produced its fruit" (James 5:17–18).

For a moment we are encouraged as we hear: "Elijah was a man with a nature like ours." Hope raises its head in expectancy when we read that, doesn't it? If Elijah was just an ordinary human being like you and me and his prayers availed much, then there is hope for us! That is, of course, until we read that this man with a nature like ours actually prayed the heavens shut for three and a half years! And it didn't end there! Elijah not only closed the heavens with prayer, he also opened them the same way.

The hope was sweet while it lasted, but it's gone. Never, never, never could we ever pray like that! "No, not me. Not an ordinary Christian like me," you may think. "That's 'super saint' praying when you pray and get answers like that!"

Is it? Was that God's intention in having James record these words? Are they meant to be words of encouragement or words of defeat? Oh, Beloved, I know they are meant to be words of hope and encouragement. What God wants us to see is that ordinary people—like you and me—can accomplish extraordinary things through prayer.

"But how?" you ask.

That's the question: "How?" And God's Word has the answer. And you and I are going to dig it out precept upon precept, line upon line, here a little and there a little, until at the end of these twenty-eight days you know exactly what it takes to make prayer effective.

A zeal for prayer is not enough. There are laws of prayer, laws laid down in God's Word. When we finish this study, we will know these laws. If you are overwhelmed by Elijah's power in prayer, think of how the disciples must have felt when they saw their Lord's powerful prayer life. That is why they said, "Lord, teach us to pray . . . " (Luke 11:1).

So, take heart. Prayer can be taught. And since it can be taught, it can be learned! That is why Jesus responded, "When you pray, say . . . " (Luke 11:2).

Take several minutes and read the following passage, Luke 11:1-10. As you read, think about why Jesus chose the illustration He uses in verses 5–8.

[1]And it came about that while He was praying in a certain place, after He had finished, one of His disciples said to Him, "Lord, teach us to pray just as John also taught his disciples." [2]And He said to them, "When you pray, say: 'Father, hallowed be Thy name. Thy kingdom come. [3]Give us each day our daily bread. [4]And forgive us our sins, for we ourselves also forgive everyone who is indebted to us. And lead us not into temptation.'" [5]And He said to them, "Suppose one

of you shall have a friend, and shall go to him at midnight, and say to him, 'Friend, lend me three loaves; [6]for a friend of mine has come to me from a journey, and I have nothing to set before him'; [7]and from inside he shall answer and say, 'Do not bother me; the door has already been shut and my children and I are in bed; I cannot get up and give you anything.' [8]I tell you, even though he will not get up and give him anything because he is his friend, yet because of his persistence he will get up and give him as much as he needs. [9]And I say to you, ask, and it shall be given to you; seek, and you shall find; knock, and it shall be opened to you. [10]For everyone who asks, receives; and he who seeks, finds; and to him who knocks, it shall be opened."

Write out why you feel Jesus used the illustration in verses 5–8.

Prayer is not easy. Prayer is a discipline, and discipline requires persistence. In this passage, the verbs *ask*, *seek*, and *knock* are all in the present tense in the Greek, which implies continuous or habitual action. Why does Jesus tell us to keep on asking, keep on seeking, keep on knocking? Why doesn't God answer our requests the very first time? Do you think that maybe it is to keep us in constant communion and to teach us persistence in the process?

If this is your prayer, echo it to our Father:

"O Lord, to be honest, I'm overwhelmed. I really wonder if I will ever be able to pray like Elijah! But, Lord, I want to learn. Teach me how to pray. Teach me the effective prayer of a righteous man that avails much. I'm going to ask and ask until it's mine. I know it's Your will. Thank You, therefore, for hearing this prayer that I ask in the name of Your Son. Amen."

Notes

"Lord, teach us to pray just as John also taught his disciples" (Luke 11:1). Oh, what precious words those are to me, for they show me that prayer is a skill that can be learned. If prayer is a skill, then it is something I can develop with time and practice.

I think we often become absolutely overwhelmed when we hear of the faith and prayer life of others. We think, "I could never attain that." So we become defeated before we ever start. Or we compare ourselves with others. We read of saints who spent hours, days, nights in prayer, and we cannot even pray for ten, twenty, or thirty minutes. How then could we ever pray for hours each day, let alone whole days or nights? We feel we will never make it, so we give up before we ever begin.

But you can attain! Just know that it will only come little by little with knowledge, with application, with time, with experience. The disciples knew this, and so they began where we each must begin if we are ever to learn—with a hunger to be taught. They had seen Jesus praying (Luke 11:1), and they knew He understood how to pray. They had a hunger to know how to pray, so they went to the Expert.

That is where you and I are going: to the Expert, the Lord Jesus Christ, the Word of God. In the context of Luke 11, Jesus answered the disciples' request by giving them what we call "the Lord's Prayer." When He gave them this prayer, did Jesus mean they were simply to say the prayer over and over? Was He saying that praying these words was the way to pray? No. For immediately before Jesus said, "Pray, then, *in this way*," He said, "When you are praying, do not use meaningless repetition" (Matthew 6:7, 9, italics added).

Therefore, the Lord's Prayer was not meant to be a prayer said by rote. Rather, Jesus was using the same manner of instruction that the rabbis of the day used. He was teaching the disciples an index for prayer. Index prayers were a collection of brief sentences, each of which suggested a subject for prayer. I believe, as do others, that the Lord's Prayer states for us in topical form the ingredients necessary for effective prayer. Nowhere else in God's Word did the disciples say to Jesus, "Teach us to pray." Nowhere else did Jesus directly say, "Pray, then, *in this way*" (Matthew 6:9, italics added). Therefore, to pray according to the index or the outline of the Lord's Prayer is to pray an effective prayer that will avail much.

Why don't you covenant before God that without fail you are going to set aside a specific time for prayer each day for the next twenty-five days? Tell Him you are coming to Him as a learner. Tell Him if He doesn't help you there is no hope! During your prayer time, talk with Him about what you have learned. Don't compare yourself with others or try to measure up to their prayer lives. It is just you and God, child and Father.

He's waiting and eager to have that time alone with you.

Notes

Wouldn't it be wonderfu! if every single principle of prayer could be condensed into several simple sentences so you could remember them easily? Then no matter where you found yourself, you could recall those principles and use them to commune with your Father in a meaningful and vital way.

Oh, Beloved, once you learn to pray, there is nothing, absolutely nothing, sweeter than knowing you have touched the hem of His garment in prayer. It's healing! It's renewing! It brings a quietness and a confidence that flows over your soul like the balm of Gilead.

But can all the truths of prayer be summarized in a few short, simple sentences? Yes! Oh, yes! They can be! They have been! Our Lord did it when He gave us the Lord's Prayer. As I said yesterday, the Lord's Prayer is a collection of index sentences, covering every element of prayer. Therefore, when you follow sentence by sentence, principle by principle, you find yourself covering every possible aspect of prayer. Every requirement for prayer, every element of worship and praise, every perspective of intercession and petition is covered in the Lord's Prayer. It is the true pattern for all prayer. Oh, what a treasure our Lord gave His disciples, and us, when they said, "Lord, teach us to pray."

Today, we will begin looking at this pattern for prayer sentence by sentence. As we look at it one precept at a time, I am going to take you to other

Scriptures which will amplify, illuminate, illustrate, or substantiate each particular precept.

I do not want you to be merely a passive reader of truth. You need to actively participate in what you are learning. Therefore, when you are asked to do something, please do it. I say that beseechingly. This is not busywork. It is a study that will help you seal truth to your heart and teach you to pray by the very doing of it! So let's begin.

The Lord's Prayer from Matthew 6:9–13 is printed out for you on the next page. Read it. Then think about it. Ask God to show you what subjects or topics for prayer are shown in this model prayer. As you read, put brackets around each sentence and then write out a title for each topic. For example:

Submission to   }   Your Title
God's will

Before you begin, let me say one very important thing: Do not be anxious about being clever or eloquent in your titles. Don't think you have to use alliteration, making all the titles begin with the same letter. That is not the point. By now you know there is nothing eloquent about my writing or my speech, yet God uses it. So relax. Let God give you insight. Then practice what you learn in prayer.

"Pray, then, in this way:

'Our Father who art in heaven,

　Hallowed be Thy name.

'Thy kingdom come.

　Thy will be done,

　On earth as it is in heaven.

'Give us this day our daily bread.

'And forgive us our debts, as we also have forgiven

　our debtors.

'And do not lead us into temptation, but deliver us

　from evil.

　[For Thine is the kingdom, and the power, and the

glory, forever. Amen.]'"

Notes

What did you see yesterday when you analyzed each of our Lord's index sentences? For the sake of continuity, let me share what I see.

TOPIC	INDEX SENTENCE	TITLE
Worship	Our Father who art in heaven, Hallowed be Thy name.	Worship of the Father
Allegiance	Thy kingdom come.	Allegiance to God's sovereignty
Submission	Thy will be done, On earth as it is in heaven.	Submission to His will
Petition and Intercession	Give us this day our daily bread.	Asking for His provision
Confession	And forgive us our debts, as we also have forgiven our debtors.	Confession and forgiveness of debts
Deliverance	And do not lead us into temptation, but deliver us from evil.	Watchfulness and deliverance
Worship	For Thine is the kingdom, and the power, and the glory, forever. Amen.	Worship

Although our titles may be worded differently, I think we can all agree that the Lord's Prayer covers these basic and all-encompassing topics. And everything God's Word says on the subject of prayer could be aligned under one of these index sentences. To pray the Lord's Prayer intelligently is to cover every topic of prayer. Therefore, if you memorize this prayer, you will have in your possession the key to effective prayer that avails much.

To help you do this, we are going to take this prayer apart sentence by sentence. Yet, we will only scratch the surface! After all, we have just twenty-three short days left! However, what we do in these twenty-three days will lay a solid foundation for your prayer life. Then you can have the joy of building the superstructure which can be as magnificent as you desire. It will depend on how much you are willing to devote yourself to prayer and to the ministry of the Word (Acts 6:4). Prayer and the Word are the essentials of Christianity. All true service for the Kingdom finds its root there.

Right now, I want you to meditate upon "Our Father who art in heaven." Why do you think Jesus began here? Think about it and write out your answer before you proceed any further. Remember, these are to be days of learning . . . learning by active participation. You will never reap more than you sow!

True prayer is nothing more and nothing less than communion with the Father. Whether you are involved in worship, intercession, petition, or thanksgiving, it is all directed to God the Father.

Hebrews 11:6 says, "And without faith it is impossible to please Him, for he who comes to God must believe that He is, and that He is a rewarder of those who seek Him." How does Hebrews 11:6 compare with Jesus' opening precept on prayer?

Did you notice that Hebrews 11:6 begins with the statement, "And without faith it is impossible to please Him"? It takes faith not only to please God, but also to come to Him. And what is faith? It is defined in Hebrews 11:1: "Faith is the *assurance* of things hoped for, the *conviction* of things not seen" (italics added).

Prayer begins by communicating with a God who, although you have never seen Him, is there—a God who "is a rewarder of those who seek Him." In light of all we have said today, can you see that the foundation, the fundamental truth of all prayer, is faith in God?

And what kind of a God is He? What is He called in Matthew 6:9? "Our Father."

Oh, Beloved, do you see it? You are not coming to some remote, untouchable, indifferent Sovereign. You are coming to a Father, a Father with children, a Father who loves, who cares, who longs to have fellowship with His children. Why don't you take a few minutes and talk to Him as a child talks to his or her father.

"But, Kay," you may say, "my father never talked to me, never cared for me, so how can I talk to God as a Father?" Even though you may have had that kind of father, didn't you long for one who was loving, affectionate, caring, and accessible? Of course you did. Well, there He is, in heaven, waiting for you to talk to Him.

Spill it all out . . . aloud. Tell Him what you think about Him as a Father. Tell Him your fears, your hopes, your expectations. Tell Him what you long for in a relationship. Then ask Him what He longs for . . . and listen carefully. Give Him time to speak; then write down what comes to your mind.

Notes

Our Father . . . what is He like? Discovering the answer to that question will greatly enhance your prayer life.

If you desire to know Him as He truly is, you must go to the Word of God. Immediately you can see why so few really know Him, can't you? We will not know our Father or His ways intimately unless we are students of His Word. We must study to show ourselves approved of God (2 Timothy 2:15). If we do not know our God and His ways, our prayer lives will be impotent and ineffective. We will not bring great things to our God in prayer unless we know how great He is. We will not ask God to move in the affairs of men in mighty ways until we understand His ways with nations and His promises regarding the affairs of men.

Let me stop here and give you an illustration. Remember how Elijah closed and opened the heavens through prayer? Awesome, wasn't it? Have you ever wondered where Elijah acquired such faith, especially if he was just an ordinary man? Well, Elijah knew the book of the Law of Moses. Elijah also knew his God. He knew that God is faithful to His Word.

When Elijah stood before wicked King Ahab and said, "As the LORD, the God of Israel lives, before whom I stand, surely there shall be neither dew nor rain these years, except by my word" (1 Kings 17:1), he was simply standing on God's Word. In Deuteronomy 28, God had stated what He would do if His people turned aside from obeying His Word. One of the things God said He would do was "make the rain of your land powder and dust . . . the heaven which is over your head shall be bronze, and the earth which is under you, iron" (Deuteronomy 28:24, 23).

Elijah was nothing special in and of himself. He was simply a man with a nature like ours. He had power in prayer because he knew his God, because he knew God's Word, and because he knew how to claim that Word in prayer. When the people repented three and a half years later, Elijah knew what to do. He prayed and claimed God's promise of rain for obedience. And it rained!

Oh, Beloved, if only we will see that the strength of our prayers begins in knowing *our Father who is in heaven* and in realizing that "every good thing bestowed and every perfect gift is from above, coming down from the Father of lights, with whom there is no variation, or shifting shadow" (James 1:17).

Let me illustrate this truth with a prayer from the Old Testament. Read 2 Chronicles 20:1–12. As you read, note what Jehoshaphat knows about his God.

[1]Now it came about after this that the sons of Moab and the sons of Ammon, together with some of the Meunites, came to make war against Jehoshaphat. [2]Then some came and reported to Jehoshaphat, saying, "A great multitude is coming against you from beyond the sea, out of Aram and behold, they are in Hazazon-tamar (that is Engedi)." [3]And Jehoshaphat was afraid and turned his attention to seek the LORD; and proclaimed a fast throughout all Judah. [4]So Judah

gathered together to seek help from the LORD; they even came from all the cities of Judah to seek the LORD. ⁵Then Jehoshaphat stood in the assembly of Judah and Jerusalem, in the house of the LORD before the new court, ⁶and he said, "O LORD, the God of our fathers, art Thou not God in the heavens? And art Thou not ruler over all the kingdoms of the nations? Power and might are in Thy hand so that no one can stand against Thee. ⁷Didst Thou not, O our God, drive out the inhabitants of this land before Thy people Israel, and give it to the descendants of Abraham Thy friend forever? ⁸And they lived in it, and have built Thee a sanctuary there for Thy name, saying, ⁹"Should evil come upon us, the sword, or judgment, or pestilence, or famine, we will stand before this house and before Thee (for Thy name is in this house) and cry to Thee in our distress, and Thou wilt hear and deliver us.' ¹⁰And now behold, the sons of Ammon and Moab and Mount Seir, whom Thou didst not let Israel invade when they came out of the land of Egypt (they turned aside from them and did not destroy them), ¹¹behold how they are rewarding us, by coming to drive us out from Thy possession which Thou hast given us as an inheritance. ¹²O our God, wilt Thou not judge them? For we are powerless before this great multitude who are coming against us; nor do we know what to do, but our eyes are on Thee" (2 Chronicles 20:1–12).

1. How does Jehoshaphat incorporate his knowledge of God into his prayer?

2. What kind of a situation provokes Jehoshaphat to prayer?

3. How does Jehoshaphat begin his prayer?

4. Do you see any parallels to the Lord's Prayer?

5. Suppose you find yourself facing an enemy. How will you pray? Can you stand firm in your knowledge of God?

6. How well do you know your Father? If you do not know Him well enough, do you realize you can do something about it? He is waiting for you in His Word.

Notes

If the Lord's Prayer is the pattern for all prayer, then through it we can learn vital truths regarding some prerequisites for effective prayer.

In the first index sentence, "Our Father who art in heaven, hallowed be Thy name," Jesus lays out two imperatives for prayer. We will look at the first of those today. (We will look at the second on Day Nine.) And as we work through the other index sentences, you will see the prerequisites for prayer.

Prayer begins with worship of the Father.

To worship someone is to acknowledge his worth, to give him the honor and reverence due him. Thus, Jesus begins by reminding us of the supremacy of God, the One who lives in the third heaven and who controls all the affairs of the universe (Daniel 4:34–35). His name is to be hallowed, to be regarded as holy, to be reverenced above all others.

Why? Because our Father is totally set apart from man. He is other than man, more than man. He is God. Thus, when you come to God in prayer, you are coming to One greater and mightier than yourself. Worship of that mighty One is the first imperative to prayer.

Remember God's commandment, "You shall not take the name of the LORD your God in vain, for the LORD will not leave him unpunished who takes His name in vain" (Exodus 20:7)? Well, the opposite of taking the Lord's name in vain is hallowing it!

"The name of the Lord denotes not merely a title, but includes all that by which He makes Himself known and all that He shows Himself to be," says one commentator.[1]

Therefore, a person can take the Lord's name in vain by disbelieving, by denying, or by distorting the truth about God.

You see, Beloved, God's names testify to His character. If you hallow His name, then you acknowledge and respect who He is and behave accordingly.

If you say, "I'm sorry, I just can't believe that God is the creator," or "I just can't believe God will really provide my needs," or "I just don't see why God would do that to a person," then you are not hallowing His name. You are taking His name in vain by thinking wrong thoughts about Him.

That is something to think about, isn't it? Many who would never think of taking the Lord's name in vain by swearing or by speaking it in a casual, slang way still desecrate His name when they doubt or deny His character.

Let me share with you some of the names of God so you may revere Him as you should (see the chart on page 40). If you have time, you will find it of great benefit to look up and write down the Scripture references where these names are used so you might see the context in which God reveals each particular aspect of His character.

---

1   Charles R. Erdman, *The Book of Exodus: An Exposition* (Grand Rapids, Michigan: Baker Book House, 1982), 95.

"Holy and reverend is his name" (Psalm 111:9 KJV). Meditate upon the names of God . . . memorize them . . . and hallow them.

Study the names of God in greater depth. To assist you in this, you may want to use the study book entitled *Lord, I Want to Know You.* I wrote this study on the names of God after I myself first studied the Lord's Prayer, for I thought, "Father, how can we fully hallow Your name if we don't know it?" Thus, that study was born, and it has been life-changing for multitudes of people because they have learned who their God is and how to approach Him in prayer. In fact, I guess of all the "Lord" studies to date this has been the book that has so transformed peoples' relationship with God that it has drawn them into all our other studies.

The stories of what God has done as individuals have made the name of the Lord their strong tower are miraculous! That's the power of His name![2]

---

2 For a more in-depth study on the names of God, you may want to order *Lord, I Want to Know You* from Precept Ministries, P.O. Box 182218, Chattanooga, Tennessee, 37422 (423-892-6814). Teaching tapes are also available, which correspond with the book and expound on what is taught in the study.

The Names of God

Name	Scripture	Means or Shows God as:
Elohim	Genesis 1:1	Creator
El Elyon	Genesis 14:18–20	The Most High (Sovereign)
Jehovah Tsidkenu	Jeremiah 23:6	The Lord our Righteousness
Jehovah Jireh	Genesis 22:14	The Lord will provide
Jehovah Raah	Psalm 23:1	The Lord my Shepherd
Jehovah Shalom	Judges 6:24	The Lord send peace
Jehovah Nissi	Exodus 17:15	The Lord my banner
Jehovah Rapha	Exodus 15:26	The Lord that healeth
Jehovah Shammah	Ezekiel 48:35	The Lord is There

Notes

We live in perilous times! Therefore, another name for God which you really need to know is "the Lord of hosts." In our day and age, many people's hearts fail them for fear, and times are going to get even worse. Those who study eschatology, the doctrine of future things, know "that in the last days difficult times will come" (2 Timothy 3:1). The hearts of men will wax colder and colder until they become haters of God and, thus, haters of the children of God. When wicked men come against us, what will we do? How will the Lord's Prayer help then?

When you are threatened, Beloved, remember His name and hallow it in prayer. Let me show you what I mean in practical terms by taking you to a marvelous illustration in the book of Isaiah. You will have to do some reading, but how you will be blessed!

Read Isaiah 36 carefully and then answer the questions that follow. Before you read this chapter, however, let me put it in context for you.

The nation of Israel has been divided into two kingdoms: the Northern Kingdom of Israel, consisting of ten tribes; and the Southern Kingdom of Judah, consisting of two tribes, Judah and Benjamin. Assyria has already taken the Northern Kingdom into captivity and is now threatening the Southern Kingdom.

[1]Now it came about in the fourteenth year of King Hezekiah, Sennacherib king of Assyria came up against all the fortified cities of Judah and seized

them. ²And the king of Assyria sent Rabshakeh from Lachish to Jerusalem to King Hezekiah with a large army. And he stood by the conduit of the upper pool on the highway of the fuller's field. ³Then Eliakim the son of Hilkiah, who was over the household, and Shebna the scribe, and Joah the son of Asaph, the recorder, came out to him. ⁴Then Rabshakeh said to them, "Say now to Hezekiah, 'Thus says the great king, the king of Assyria, "What is this confidence that you have? ⁵I say, 'Your counsel and strength for the war are only empty words.' Now on whom do you rely, that you have rebelled against me? ⁶Behold, you rely on the staff of this crushed reed, even on Egypt; on which if a man leans, it will go into his hand and pierce it. So is Pharaoh king of Egypt to all who rely on him. ⁷But if you say to me, 'We trust in the LORD our God,' is it not He whose high places and whose altars Hezekiah has taken away, and has said to Judah and to Jerusalem, 'You shall worship before this altar'? ⁸Now therefore, come make a bargain with my master the king of Assyria, and I will give you two thousand horses, if you are able on your part to set riders on them. ⁹How then can you repulse one official of the least of my master's servants, and rely on Egypt for chariots and for horsemen? ¹⁰And have I now come up without the LORD's approval against this land to destroy it? The LORD said to me, 'Go up against this land, and destroy it.'"'" ¹¹Then Eliakim and Shebna and Joah said to Rabshakeh, "Speak now to your servants in Aramaic, for we understand it; and do not speak with us in Judean, in the hearing of the people who are on the wall." ¹²But Rabshakeh said, "Has my master sent me only to your master and to you to speak these words, and not to the men who sit on the wall, doomed to eat their own dung and drink their own urine with you?" ¹³Then Rabshakeh stood and cried with a loud voice in Judean, and said, "Hear the words of the great king, the king of Assyria. [14]Thus says the king, 'Do not let Hezekiah deceive you, for he will not be able to deliver you; [15]nor let Hezekiah make you trust in the LORD, saying, "The LORD will surely deliver us, this city shall not be given into the hand of the king of Assyria." [16]Do not listen to Hezekiah,' for thus says the king of Assyria, 'Make your peace with me and come out to me, and eat each of his vine and each of his fig tree and drink each of the waters of his own cistern, [17]until I come and take you away to a land like your own land, a land of grain and new wine, a land of bread and vineyards. [18]Beware lest Hezekiah misleads you, saying, "The LORD will deliver us." Has any one of the gods of the nations delivered his land from the hand of the king of Assyria? [19]Where are the gods of Hamath and Arpad? Where are the gods of Sepharvaim? And when have they delivered Samaria from my hand? [20]Who among all the gods of these lands have delivered their land from my hand, that the LORD should deliver Jerusalem from my hand?'" [21]But they were silent and answered him not a word; for the king's commandment was, "Do not answer him." [22]Then Eliakim the son of Hilkiah, who was over the household, and Shebna the scribe and Joah the son of Asaph, the recorder, came to Hezekiah with their clothes torn and told him the words of Rabshakeh (Isaiah 36).

1. Who is Rabshakeh?

2. What is he threatening?

3. According to Isaiah 36:10, who has sanctioned what he is doing?

4. According to Isaiah 36:18–20, what is Rabshakeh's attitude toward God?

Now read Isaiah 37 and answer the questions that follow. How I love this chapter!

¹And when King Hezekiah heard it, he tore his clothes, covered himself with sackcloth and entered the house of the LORD. ²Then he sent Eliakim who was over the household with Shebna the scribe and the elders of the priests, covered with sackcloth, to Isaiah the prophet, the son of Amoz. ³And they said to him, "Thus says Hezekiah, 'This day is a day of distress, rebuke, and rejection; for children have come to birth, and there is no strength to deliver. ⁴Perhaps the LORD your God will hear the words of Rabshakeh, whom his master the king of Assyria has sent to reproach the living God, and will rebuke the words which the LORD your God has heard. Therefore, offer a prayer for the remnant that is left.'" ⁵So the servants of King Hezekiah came to Isaiah. ⁶And Isaiah said to them, "Thus you shall say to your master, 'Thus says the LORD, "Do not be afraid because of the words that you have heard, with which

the servants of the king of Assyria have blasphemed Me. [7]Behold, I will put a spirit in him so that he shall hear a rumor and return to his own land. And I will make him fall by the sword in his own land." ' " [8]Then Rabshakeh returned and found the king of Assyria fighting against Libnah, for he had heard that the king had left Lachish. [9]When he heard them say concerning Tirhakah king of Cush, "He has come out to fight against you," and when he heard it he sent messengers to Hezekiah, saying, [10]"Thus you shall say to Hezekiah king of Judah, 'Do not let your God in whom you trust deceive you, saying, "Jerusalem shall not be given into the hand of the king of Assyria." [11]Behold, you have heard what the kings of Assyria have done to all the lands, destroying them completely. So will you be spared? [12]Did the gods of those nations which my fathers have destroyed deliver them, even Gozan and Haran and Rezeph and the sons of Eden who were in Telassar? [13]Where is the king of Hamath, the king of Arpad, the king of the city of Sepharvaim, and of Hena and Ivvah?' " [14]Then Hezekiah took the letter from the hand of the messengers and read it, and he went up to the house of the LORD and spread it out before the LORD. [15]And Hezekiah prayed to the LORD saying, [16]"O LORD of hosts, the God of Israel, who art enthroned above the cherubim, Thou art the God, Thou alone, of all the kingdoms of the earth. Thou hast made heaven and earth. [17]Incline Thine ear, O LORD, and hear; open Thine eyes, O LORD, and see; and listen to all the words of Sennacherib, who sent them to reproach the living God. [18]Truly, O LORD, the kings of Assyria have devastated all the countries and their lands, [19]and have cast their gods into the fire, for they were not gods but the work of men's hands, wood and stone. So they have destroyed them. [20]And now, O

LORD our God, deliver us from his hand that all the
kingdoms of the earth may know that Thou alone,
LORD, art God." 21Then Isaiah the son of Amoz sent
word to Hezekiah, saying, "Thus says the LORD, the
God of Israel, 'Because you have prayed to Me about
Sennacherib king of Assyria, 22this is the word that
the LORD has spoken against him: "She has despised
you and mocked you, the virgin daughter of Zion; she
has shaken her head behind you, the daughter of
Jerusalem! 23Whom have you reproached and blasphemed? And against whom have you raised your
voice, and haughtily lifted up your eyes? Against the
Holy One of Israel! 24Through your servants you
have reproached the Lord, and you have said, 'With
my many chariots I came up to the heights of the
mountains, to the remotest parts of Lebanon; and I
cut down its tall cedars and its choice cypresses. And
I will go to its highest peak, its thickest forest. 25I dug
wells and drank waters, and with the sole of my feet
I dried up all the rivers of Egypt.' 26Have you not
heard? Long ago I did it, from ancient times I planned
it. Now I have brought it to pass, that you should turn
fortified cities into ruinous heaps. 27Therefore their
inhabitants were short of strength, they were dis-
mayed and put to shame; they were as the vegetation
of the field and as the green herb, as grass on the
housetops is scorched before it is grown up. 28But I
know your sitting down, and your going out and your
coming in, and your raging against Me. 29Because of
your raging against Me, and because your arrogance
has come up to My ears, therefore I will put My hook
in your nose, and My bridle in your lips, and I will
turn you back by the way which you came. 30Then
this shall be the sign for you: you shall eat this year
what grows of itself, in the second year what springs
from the same, and in the third year sow, reap, plant

vineyards, and eat their fruit. [31]And the surviving remnant of the house of Judah shall again take root downward and bear fruit upward. [32]For out of Jerusalem shall go forth a remnant, and out of Mount Zion survivors. The zeal of the LORD of hosts shall perform this." ' [33]Therefore, thus says the LORD concerning the king of Assyria, 'He shall not come to this city, or shoot an arrow there; neither shall he come before it with a shield, nor throw up a mound against it. [34]By the way that he came, by the same he shall return, and he shall not come to this city,' declares the LORD. [35]'For I will defend this city to save it for My own sake and for My servant David's sake.'" [36]Then the angel of the LORD went out, and struck 185,000 in the camp of the Assyrians; and when men arose early in the morning, behold, all of these were dead. [37]So Sennacherib, king of Assyria, departed and returned home, and lived at Nineveh. [38]And it came about as he was worshiping in the house of Nisroch his god, that Adrammelech and Sharezer his sons killed him with the sword; and they escaped into the land of Ararat. And Esarhaddon his son became king in his place (Isaiah 37).

1. What does Hezekiah do when he hears Rabshakeh's words?

2. What does this tell you about Hezekiah?

3. Note once again Rabshakeh's attitude toward God in Isaiah 37:8–13.

4. In Isaiah 37:14–15, what does Hezekiah do with the letter of Rabshakeh?

Go back to Isaiah 37:16–20 and look at Hezekiah's prayer to God. Read it again and then answer the questions that follow.

1. How does Hezekiah hallow God's name?

2. What parallels do you see between this prayer and the Lord's Prayer?

What did you learn today that you can apply to your life?

Notes

Two days ago we looked at the first imperative for prayer found in the first index sentence of the Lord's Prayer. That first imperative was worship. Today we will look at the second imperative found in that same index sentence. But first there is one more thing I want to share with you regarding worship.

In the Scripture when you find people worshiping the Godhead, you never find them repeating the same phrases over and over again, such as, "Praise You, Jesus; praise You, Jesus."

Oh, in Isaiah 6 you find the seraphim calling out, "Holy, holy, holy, is the LORD of hosts . . ." (Isaiah 6:3 KJV). However, a threefold repetition simply was the way of denoting the ultimate of a truth, such as the holiness of God. A twofold repetition such as, "verily, verily" simply established the veracity of something.

In biblical worship you do not find the repetition of a phrase; instead, you find the worshipers rehearsing the character of God and His ways, reminding Him of His faithfulness and His wonderful promises. The heathen often worked themselves up through excited and frenzied repetition of a phrase in the worship of their gods, but with the children of God this was not so!

We do not need vain repetition. Our worship is based on truth, not emotion; it is based not on the fervency of our words, but on the faithfulness of our God. Emotion follows truth!

Turn to the following prayers in your Bible. As you read them, note *how* the petitioner worships God. By that I mean, what does he say about God? How does he approach God?

Jeremiah 32:16–25

Daniel 2:19–23

Daniel 9:3–19

Which do you think is more beneficial in worship: a) simply repeating "Praise You, Jesus" over and over, or b) rehearsing the character, the ways, and the promises of your God? Which takes a greater familiarity with God and His Word? If you were the one being worshiped, which would you prefer? Remember, to worship means to acknowledge another's worth. Which form of worship does this more effectively?

Think about this in the light of His Word and then worship your God accordingly.

Now, let's look at the second imperative for prayer: the Fatherhood of God.

According to God's Word, no man, woman, or child can call God "Father" apart from Jesus, for until we are born again God is not our Father (John 3:5). "But as many as received Him [Jesus Christ], to them He gave the right to become children of God, even to those who believe in His name, who were born not of blood, nor of the will of the flesh, nor of the will of man, but of God" (John 1:12–13).

Not until you receive the Lord Jesus Christ do you become a child of God. However, once you receive Him as your Lord and Savior, you are then sealed with the Holy Spirit.[3] The Holy Spirit is given to you at salvation and is the guarantee of the redemption of your body. The redemption of your body means you will have a brand-new body someday (1 Corinthians 15:51–54). Carefully read Ephesians 1:13–14, noting what you see about the Holy Spirit.

In Him, you also, after listening to the message of truth, the gospel of your salvation—having also believed, you were sealed in Him with the Holy Spirit of promise, who is given as a pledge of our

---

3   The two, Savior and Lord, cannot be separated. If you think so, look up every Scripture that relates to salvation and see if the title Lord is used. Or use your concordance and count the times Lord is used. Then count the times Savior is used apart from Lord and look up the references.

inheritance, with a view to the redemption of God's own possession, to the praise of His glory (Ephesians 1:13–14).

Let me give you one last Scripture which confirms it is only through salvation and the gift of the Holy Spirit that you can call God "Father."

For all who are being led by the Spirit of God, these are sons of God. . . . you have received a spirit of adoption as sons by which we cry out, "Abba! Father!" (Romans 8:14–15).

Oh, Beloved, do you realize what all this means? It means that prayer is a privilege reserved for those who are truly the children of God. Prayer is not for the masses. Prayer is only for those who can say with Jesus, "Our Father . . . ." This is the second imperative for prayer. Think on it. What significance does this have for your life?

I've had people share with me that one of the ways they discovered they had a religion rather than a relationship was the fact that they never really had direct answers to prayer.

Many are in exactly this state and my heart aches for them. The "something" that seems to be missing in their Christian experience, leaving it lifeless and routine, is really Someone—the blessed indwelling Holy Spirit!

And how do you know if He is there—living within? You know because there's a change. A Christian is a new creation.

If you have questions about the certainty of your salvation, Beloved, look up the following Scriptures: 2 Corinthians 5:17; Ephesians 1:13–15; 1 John 2:3–6; 1 John 3:7–10; 1 Corinthians 6:9–11; and 1 John 5:11–14.

As you read these passages, ask God to speak to your heart and then write down your observations. Ask Him to show you where you stand in respect to Him. You can have every confidence that He will, because He desires that you know truth, and He says that if you will seek Him and search for Him with all your heart, you will be found of Him.

What is the Spirit of God saying to you? Remember, He never condemns. It's not His will that you perish, but that you believe.

Notes

"Thy kingdom come," the second index sentence, is potent in its brevity. What does it mean? Why is it a topic for prayer? Why is it separate from, "Thy will be done, on earth as it is in heaven"?

For a while I could not see why these two sentences had to be separated. It took meditation to gain understanding. How I wish I had several days to share all that is contained in these three words, "Thy kingdom come"! However, since we have limited this study to twenty-eight days, let me share the essence of what I believe our Lord is saying; then you can take it deeper. But do take it deeper. Meditate on it, for it is a truth greatly lacking in the body of Christ.

"Thy kingdom come" is a confirmation in prayer of our allegiance to the sovereign rule of the Kingdom of God above all else. Prayer is simply communication with God, talking with the Sovereign Ruler of all the universe. As we have seen, this communication begins with worship, an acknowledgment of the truth about our Father, a hallowing or reverencing of His name. His name, of course, reveals His person! From worship, then, we are to move to allegiance.

Allegiance? Aren't worship and allegiance synonymous? You tell me. Do you know people who acknowledge the "worthship" of God yet who are not fully aligned with His Kingdom and its preeminence? I do. I know people who stand and extol who God is; yet even though they know and confess Him properly, they are still more concerned about the furtherance of their ministry, their denomination, their pet doctrine, their legalistic set of dos and don'ts, their own comfort and welfare than they are concerned about the furtherance of His Kingdom. I know people who say, "I know I should study God's Word more," or "I know I should witness," or "I know I should be more involved in His work but . . . ." But! But what? What they are actually saying is, "But my first allegiance is not to God." Think about it.

Now, your next question may be, as mine was, "But doesn't this fit right in with submission to His will when we pray, 'Thy will be done'"? Yes, Beloved, the two go together. But true, complete, absolute submission to God's will is born only out of undivided, absolute allegiance to His Kingdom.

And this is where the church of Jesus Christ has fallen flat on its face in the mud of the world! We are double-minded, desiring the best of both worlds, forgetting that "our citizenship is in heaven, from which also we eagerly wait for a Savior, the Lord Jesus Christ" (Philippians 3:20). We are not eagerly awaiting Him because we have entangled ourselves in allegiances that keep us from seeking "first His kingdom and His righteousness" (Matthew 6:33).

Our allegiances are to money and what it provides, to position and its prestige, to things and their pleasures, to "churchianity" and its works. Notice I say churchianity, not Christianity. Churchianity puts the church first; Christianity puts Christ first. We forget Christ is the head of the church! We give lip service to God. We want only enough of Christianity to get us to heaven, only enough to get our prayers answered. We do not want to give total allegiance to His Kingdom. We do not want His Kingdom to come today, tomorrow, or even within a few years because, like Demas, we love this present world more (2 Timothy 4:10).

As I write this, truth is "in my heart . . . like a burning fire shut up in my bones" (Jeremiah 20:9). Oh, how my heart grieves as I see multitudes across our country who name His name yet who have not given Him their total allegiance.

"You are judging!" you might say. No, Beloved, I am discerning. Our fruit, or sparseness of it, bears witness to our allegiance. When men and women have time for everything except a personal, diligent study of God's Word, I know they are not approved unto God (2 Timothy 2:15). They know much about the world but little about God! Why? Because they have time for the things of this life but not time to study God's Word. They refuse to believe that "man does not live by bread alone, but . . . by everything that proceeds out of the mouth of the LORD" (Deuteronomy 8:3)! Communion with God through His Word and prayer is essential to the fruitful life that will hasten the coming of His Kingdom.

When Jesus called men and women to Himself, what kind of allegiance did He ask for? Carefully read the following Scriptures.

And He summoned the multitude with His disciples, and said to them, "If anyone wishes to come after Me,

let him deny himself, and take up his cross, and
follow Me" (Mark 8:34).

"If anyone comes to Me, and does not hate his own
father and mother and wife and children and brothers
and sisters, yes, and even his own life, he cannot be
My disciple" (Luke 14:26).

"Do not think that I came to bring peace on the earth;
I did not come to bring peace, but a sword. For I came
to SET A MAN AGAINST HIS FATHER, AND A DAUGH-
TER AGAINST HER MOTHER, AND A DAUGHTER-IN-
LAW AGAINST HER MOTHER-IN-LAW; and A MAN'S
ENEMIES WILL BE THE MEMBERS OF HIS HOUSE-
HOLD. He who loves father or mother more than Me
is not worthy of Me; and he who loves son or daughter
more than Me is not worthy of Me. And he who does
not take his cross and follow after Me is not worthy
of Me. He who has found his life shall lose it, and he
who has lost his life for My sake shall find it" (Matthew 10:34–39).

Write out your understanding of the allegiance
Jesus asks for.

Anything less than denying yourself, taking up your cross, and following Him (Mark 8:34), than hating your own father and mother and husband and wife and children and brothers and sisters, yes, and even your own life is divided allegiance, and anything less will not allow you to honestly pray, "Thy kingdom come." Let me share one last passage of Scripture for you to meditate upon.

And as they were going along the road, someone said to Him, "I will follow You wherever You go." And Jesus said to him, "The foxes have holes, and the birds of the air have nests, but the Son of Man has nowhere to lay His head." And He said to another, "Follow Me." But he said, "Permit me first to go and bury my father." But He said to him, "Allow the dead to bury their own dead; but as for you, go and proclaim everywhere the kingdom of God." And another also said, "I will follow You, Lord; but first permit me to say good-bye to those at home." But Jesus said to him, "No one, after putting his hand to the plow and looking back, is fit for the kingdom of God" (Luke 9:57–62).

Did you notice the phrases "permit me first" and "but first permit me"? What was Jesus' response to these excuses or delays? In essence it was, "No." His Kingdom must have the preeminence "so that He Himself might come to have first place in everything" (Colossians 1:18).

Therefore, when you pray, pray, "Thy kingdom come." And as you pray, examine yourself to see if there is anything in your heart that is keeping you from undivided allegiance to the hastening of the coming of His Kingdom.

I have a little more to say on this second index sentence, but I will leave it for our twenty-first day together. For now, why don't you go to our Father and ask Him to show you anything that is dividing or dissipating your allegiance to His Kingdom? Write it out.

Confess this to a close and faithful friend in the Lord, and together seek God in prayer. For, "Two are better than one because they have a good return for their labor. For if either of them falls, the one will lift up his companion. But woe to the one who falls when there is not another to lift him up" (Ecclesiastes 4:9–10).

Notes

For the next few days we are going to look at the implications of the third topic for prayer: submission to the will of God.

According to the Lord's Prayer, true prayer is submission to the will of the Father: "Thy will be done on earth as it is in heaven." Is that merely a prayer only to be fulfilled when Jesus returns and "the sovereignty, the dominion, and the greatness of all the kingdoms under the whole heaven will be given to the people of the saints of the Highest One" . . . when "all the dominions will serve and obey Him" (Daniel 7:27)?

No, Beloved. "Thy will be done" is not a prayer to pray as we wait for the coming Kingdom; it is a heart attitude of *present* submission to the *present* sovereignty and will of the Father.

The will of the Father is that you believe on the Son, the Lord Jesus Christ, God incarnate (John 6:40). Incarnate means "in the flesh." In other words, the Father's will is that you believe Jesus Christ is God come in the flesh. Not to believe this truth is to die in your sins (John 8:24). Those who do not believe in the Lord Jesus Christ are going against the will of God and, therefore, remain dead in trespasses and sins (Ephesians 2:1). The wrath of God abides on them (John 3:36), for "there is salvation in no one else; for there is no other name under heaven that has been given among men, by which we must be saved" (Acts 4:12).

Submission to God is an integral part of salvation. To believe that Jesus is God is to acknowledge His position and rights as God. To recognize Him as Savior is to see that only this God-man can save you from your sins. And what is the root of all sin? Is it not independence? Is it not self having its own way? Isaiah 53:6 says that like sheep we have turned each "to his own way." If you look up each of the verses that actually define sin, you discover that each verse shows to one degree or another that we have willfully chosen to break the law, to not believe, to choose *our* path rather than God's.

Remember on Day Nine when you were told to look up some Scriptures that would show you what the evidences of salvation are? Well, one of the evidences of salvation is a willingness to submit to God: to recognize that because He is God and you are man, you are to submit to Him. So before we pursue this attitude of submission in respect to prayer, let's look at the relationship of submission and salvation.

Look up the following verses and note what you learn from them.

Matthew 7:18–27

1 John 5:3–5

Now, look up John 9:31, write it out below, and then think about what it says.

Does it help you better understand the relationship between submission to God and answered prayer?

Oh, Beloved, are you still in your sins, or are you a worshiper of God who longs to do the will of the Father? Only the latter has access to God in prayer.

Notes

Several years ago a dear brother in the Lord visited Precept Ministries for the first time. Since he also had a television ministry, he was anxious to see our studio and equipment. As we talked about cameras, I said, "I only wish the Lord would give us a third camera." Immediately he responded, lovingly and adamantly, "Quit wishing. Believe you have it and it's yours. Just say, 'I believe,' and it's done."

Could I say, "I believe" and know it's done? Because we had not received that third camera at that time, was I lacking in faith? Is a positive confession of faith all it takes to get our prayers answered? Precept Ministries' staff and faithful prayer warriors had been praying for that third camera for a number of years. Did we miss the camera because we did not say, "I believe"? My dear brother said he had been confessing his second camera for two years. (By the way, although he was believing and confessing, he did not have his camera either.) While we are talking about this, let's go back to our discussion on Day One regarding Debra's prayer for the woman with terminal cancer. Could that person be healed if only we believed and confessed that belief in prayer?

Many say, "Yes." To support their stand, they quote Scripture and tell many case histories of those who were healed after they and their loved ones had made a positive confession of faith. Some of the Scriptures they quote are: "If ye shall ask any thing in my name, I will do it" (John 14:14 KJV). "Hitherto have ye asked nothing in my name: ask, and ye shall receive, that your joy may be full" (John 16:24 KJV). "If ye have faith as a grain of mustard seed, ye shall say unto this mountain, Remove hence to yonder place; and it shall remove; and nothing shall be impossible unto you" (Matthew 17:20 KJV). "Therefore I say unto you, What things soever ye desire, when ye pray, believe that ye receive them, and ye shall have them" (Mark 11:24 KJV).

Are those Scriptures true? Can they be trusted? Do they have to do with prayer? Of course! The answer to all three of those questions must be in the affirmative, for God's Word is inerrant, without error.

Then my friend was right, wasn't he? All I had to do, all Debra had to do, was believe, confess it in prayer, and it would be done. What do you think? Why do you take the stand that you do? What is the scriptural basis of your stand?

Think on these things. It's vital. Put your answer on paper. Talk to the Father. We will talk about it tomorrow.

Notes

Have you ever been embarrassed or even afraid to pray for things in a definite way for fear God wouldn't answer your prayer? I have. I have thought, "Father, what if You don't answer this prayer? It's going to look like prayer doesn't work!" At this point some of you may be laughing at me . . . I don't blame you, because I'm laughing too! I can hear you saying, "Kay, why put the blame on God if the prayer is not answered? Why not put it on yourself?"

I'll tell you why! I felt I was claiming faith in His character and His ways and if God didn't come through, it really would look like He had failed! Honestly! That is the way I felt. Let me give you an illustration. This one is from my early days as a Christian, when I was about three or four years old in the Lord. Since then I have come to trust my Father more and to relax in His ways.

Jack and I were missionaries in Mexico and had taken a group of English-speaking teens on a week-end retreat. Conditions were really primitive, but the girls had the best end of the deal. We had an army surplus tent over our heads.

That night as we sat around the campfire and I taught, God really spoke. Several missionary kids who thought they were saved came to the Lord that evening. I am wary of emotional decisions around campfires, so I did not offer an invitation. Even so, from out of the dark they came to me, separately, many in tears, telling me they had turned to God and were willing to follow Him totally. God had moved! (Time eventually proved the reality of these commitments.)

Well, you can imagine the joy in the tent that night. You know how girls are! They were at fever pitch when all of a sudden we heard a loud, agonized, "Oh, no! I've dropped my contact! My parents will kill me." Now you know missionary parents are not allowed to kill their children because it's a bad testimony! However, Gail was probably right—it might have crossed their minds. The lost contact was a brand-new one she had gotten to replace another one she had just lost! Replacing contacts is hard on missionary support funds!

At any rate, we were all down on our knees with lanterns held above our heads as we looked in green grass for a green-tinted contact! And at that moment God reminded me that I had just been teaching these teens about Him, His attributes, and His ways. "Ask Me to find it," came the thought. "Ask Me in front of the girls."

A silent debate ensued. "But, Father, what if I ask You and we don't find it? How is that going to look?" I went back to my groping, but I couldn't help thinking, "He does know where it is because He is omniscient, all-knowing. There is not a thing hidden from His sight." Still I resisted; it was too risky. We might not find it. Then how would God look? I had better not risk His reputation in front of ones so young in the faith. (Can you understand what I was going through?)

Well, God won. I prayed. As I did, I reminded Him fervently of every promise I could think of that related to our plight.

After I finished, we continued to search for a while to the intermittent tune of Gail's swan song, one short chorus, "My parents are gonna kill me! My parents are gonna kill me!"

When I was almost ready to tell God I never should have prayed aloud, Lily let out a hysterical yelp, "I found it! I found it!" Tears poured down her face. But why? These weren't gushy, sentimental, girlish tears.

I didn't have to wait long to find out. Of all the teens, none was more exemplary in behavior or zeal for missions than Lily. Any one of us would have willingly claimed her as our own. She would have made us look like ideal missionary parents! Lily claimed to have been saved at a very young age, and her behavior gave us no cause to doubt the reality of her profession. Yet here was that precious girl, tears streaming down her face, half-laughing and half-crying as she told us her story.

After the lesson around the campfire, Lily realized she really had never been saved. It was hard for her to believe since she had led so many others to Christ. Yet she knew it was true, so there in the dark the transaction had taken place. Lily had passed from death to life, from the power of Satan to the Kingdom of God. She had received forgiveness of sins and an inheritance among those who are sanctified (Acts 26:18). She had been coming into the tent to tell us when Gail went into hysterics over her contact.

While I was on my knees looking for the contact and wrestling with God about praying aloud, Lily was praying: "O God, You have never directly answered my prayers all these years. Now that I am Yours, prove it by answering this prayer. Let me find Gail's contact."

Does God always find lost contacts when we pray? I know of some cases where He hasn't, even though those who prayed sincerely believed. Why did He find Gail's? Because I believed? No. Because it was His will—and in this instance we prayed according to His will.

Think on it. Pray about it. The will of God is a key to solving many mysteries regarding prayer. What have you been asking God for? Did you ask Him first if it was His will? If not, then why don't you spend time in prayer asking Him to show you His will?

Notes

So on the one hand we have "just believing" and on the other we have "the will of God." How do we relate both to effective prayer? This is a valid question. Finding the answer will liberate you from the general, safe, "God bless everyone" type of praying. Once you grasp this truth, it will stop you from brash prayers that often discredit God in the eyes of men, and it will release you to pray in confidence for specific things.

At the risk of being redundant, let's go back to Jesus' instructions on how to pray:

1. Prayer is for those who can and will say, "Our Father who art in heaven, hallowed be Thy name." Prayer is only effective for those who have become the children of God through believing on the Lord Jesus Christ. To pray a prayer that gets results, you must be a worshiper of the One to whom you are praying.

2. Prayer requires allegiance to His Kingdom—being fully aligned with God's Kingdom and its preeminence above all else.

3. Prayer requires submission: a willingness to do His will, whatever it might be, here and now on earth. "Thy kingdom come. Thy will be done on earth *as it is in heaven*." There is no adjusting God's will just because we live on an earth that does not acknowledge His rule.

Now, in the light of this third index statement, which calls for submission to the will of God, can I simply pray or ask for anything and expect it to happen? Will it happen just because I am a child of God and because I believe, ask, and am willing to make a positive confession of faith? What if my prayer is *not* the will of God?

For the purpose of illustration, what if it wasn't God's will for us to have a third camera? And what if, in faith, I confessed that God was going to give us the camera in the next sixty days? Suppose I thought I had a good reason, such as saving us from throwing God's money away by renting equipment? As a child of God, did I have the privilege to claim the third camera? Could I, in my "simply believe and confess" prayers, believe and confess within time limits? If it is only a matter of believe and confess, why not? Think about it!

Oh, Beloved, I know people who have been severely shipwrecked in their faith because they set time limits on God. They claimed a Scripture, set the date, and when it didn't come to pass they nearly fell apart. Others have believed and confessed a loved one's physical healing—only to have the person die.

One dear woman told me she knew God would heal her father. When he died on his hospital bed, she laid her Bible on his chest and prayed him back to life. Sometime later he died a second time. Once again she forbade the hospital staff to do anything to his body. She shut the door to his room and for five or six hours commanded him to live because she had believed. She was clinging to the truths of Matthew 21:21–22:

And Jesus answered and said to them, "Truly I say to you, if you have faith, and do not doubt, you shall not only do what was done to the fig tree, but even if you say to this mountain, 'Be taken up and cast into the sea,' it shall happen. And all things you ask in prayer, believing, you shall receive."

But what about 1 John 5:14–15?

And this is the confidence which we have before Him, that, if we ask anything according to His will, He hears us. And if we know that He hears us in whatever we ask, we know that we have the requests which we have asked from Him.

How does the reference in 1 John compare with Matthew 21:21–22? Write out your insights, and we'll share more tomorrow.

Notes

Those who believe that Christ's death not only bought our redemption from sin but also purchased the complete healing of our bodies are great proponents of the "believe, confess, and it's yours" type of praying. Some refer to it as a "faith message." They say believing is not enough—you must have faith. They distinguish faith from belief by saying that faith is acting on what you believe. Belief is passive; faith is active. A positive confession activates belief. What you say is what you get. Therefore, negative confessions are a lack of faith. You are not believing God. Thus, God cannot answer your prayer.

How do they biblically support this teaching? I cannot begin to touch on all their proof texts. However, one major Scripture reference is in Matthew 21 which you looked at in part yesterday.

Read Matthew 21:18–22 and mark the following words: *faith, doubt, believe (believing), say.*

Now in the morning, when He returned to the city, He became hungry. And seeing a lone fig tree by the road, He came to it, and found nothing on it except leaves only; and He said to it, "No longer shall there ever be any fruit from you." And at once the fig tree withered. And seeing this, the disciples marveled, saying, "How did the fig tree wither at once?" And

Jesus answered and said to them, "Truly I say to you,
if you have faith, and do not doubt, you shall not only
do what was done to the fig tree, but even if you say
to this mountain, 'Be taken up and cast into the sea,'
it shall happen. And all things you ask in prayer,
believing, you shall receive" (Matthew 21:18–22).

They also use Mark 11:23–24, which essentially
says the same thing. Mark the same words as you read.

"Truly I say to you, whoever says to this mountain,
'Be taken up and cast into the sea,' and does not
doubt in his heart, but believes that what he says is
going to happen, it shall be granted him. Therefore I
say to you, all things for which you pray and ask,
believe that you have received them, and they shall
be granted you" (Mark 11:23–24).

If you took these verses from Matthew and Mark
and isolated them from the rest of Scripture, then you
could make them support a "believe, confess, and
you've got it" theology. And according to these texts,
if it didn't work, you could say it was because of
doubt. It would be an open-and-shut case.

But, Beloved, you cannot isolate Scripture. All Scripture must agree. Scripture cannot contradict Scripture!

Therefore, if you are going to understand the true nature of prayer and all of its workings, you must know all that the Word of God teaches on the subject! That is why you cannot take John 14:14, "If ye shall ask any thing in my name, I will do it" (KJV), and run with it! To do so will be disastrous.

I want to take just a few minutes and illustrate what I am saying through a letter I received from a woman who was caught up in this teaching.

> I wanted to write . . . to say thank you for the devotional on October 15 in *Beloved*. In fact, thank you doesn't seem strong enough. Maybe I should say THANK YOU!!!!!!!!
>
> I praise God that He has given you the boldness to speak out against the faith-and-positive confession teaching that is so prevalent. Yes, this teaching IS doing "grave harm"—I still have the scars. And, while you nor I have the time for me to tell you my life story, I'll just say that I know what it is to be a new Christian just ready and totally willing to begin the long journey toward deeper and deeper surrender to the Lord and His perfect will and then to be hit with this teaching. I know what it is to break fellowship with Christian groups and leaders and friends because you're under condemnation for having a cold. I know how lonely it can feel to be going through a time of physical or mental or spiritual struggle and need someone to talk to—but you can't talk to anyone because you may be accused of a negative confession. I know how it hurts to want to surrender to the Lord you love—to want to surrender to His will with all your heart, but to be told that if you do that you're opening the door to the devil. That

if you pray "Thy will be done," you're showing a dangerous lack of faith and allowing the devil to get a toehold. As though the devil has such power that you have to stay on your toes day and night to keep your healing, etc. As though your faith were in your faith rather than in the Almighty, All Powerful, All Loving, All Holy, All Just God.

It hurts me, Kay. It hurts to see Christians with this view of God that I now know is distorted. It hurts to see Christians demand things of their Father like spoiled children, and then turn and be actually hostile to those who "don't have enough faith" to believe like they do. How it must grieve our dear Lord Jesus when He sees us behave this way.

And I have been guilty of it as much as any, for I "bought into" this distorted teaching for a while (I figured that if all these "spiritual giants" believed it, it must be true). I not only know what it is to be looked down upon because of my lack of faith, I also know what it is to pass off a person in need with a "well, it's obvious she's sick/grieved/depressed/angry/etc. because she's not right with the Lord and she's confessing negatively." It can become quite a science. And quite a sin.

Lord, forgive us. Lord, teach us to love.

Did you notice, "if all these 'spiritual giants' believed it, it must be true"? Where does your theology come from? Do you believe because of men's teachings and experiences or because you have dug out truth from God's Word yourself, precept upon precept?

Sometimes what happens, Beloved, is that we simply accept teaching because we love, admire, and/or trust our teachers—and that is wonderful if the teachers are correct in all they teach. However, we forget that no one person has a corner on all the truth. Therefore, we need to be like the Bereans who, after the apostle Paul taught, searched the Scriptures to see whether or not what he taught was in keeping with the Word.

Those who believe that healing is for everyone often cite Isaiah 53:4–5 as a proof text, saying that "physical healing is part of the atonement." By that they mean that Christ's death won our healing and, therefore, we only have to claim it in believing prayer or confession.

Since the Word of God plays such a critical role in prayer because it shows us the will of God, it might be profitable for us to take a few minutes and look at Isaiah 53:4–5 and let Scripture interpret Scripture. Remember, Scripture is the best interpreter of Scripture and the final word. Who are we to contradict God!

Isaiah 53:4–5 says:

> Surely our griefs He Himself bore, and our sorrows He carried; yet we ourselves esteemed Him stricken, smitten of God, and afflicted. But He was pierced through for our transgressions, He was crushed for our iniquities; the chastening for our well-being *fell* upon Him, and by His scourging we are healed.

In Matthew 8:14–17 we find the correct interpretation of Isaiah 53:4. Look up the verses. You may want to write them out.

Now, read through the verses again, this time in-
terrogating the text with any of the 5 W's and an H
which are appropriate: who, what, when, where, why,
and how. For example, who are the main characters
in this incident? What is happening? When is it taking
place (that is, after Christ's death, during His cruci-
fixion, or during His public ministry)? Where is it
occurring? Why does God tell us what He does in
verse 17? How did the healing take place?

By the way, you may want to write Matthew 8:14–17 in your Bible next to Isaiah 53:4, and then do the same cross-referencing by writing Isaiah 53:4 in the margin beside Matthew 8:14–17.

Now look up 1 Peter 2:24–25 and cross-reference it with Isaiah 53:5. Again ask the appropriate 5 W's and an H and record your insights. As you read the verses in 1 Peter, note what we are healed of and when and how.

We could look up other verses in respect to healing, but that is not our purpose in this book. I did not have you do this for the sake of controversy but simply to help you in this aspect of prayer, because it can be so discouraging to pray for someone's healing and not see him or her physically healed.

I went through this with my precious father. I knew without a shadow of a doubt that God could heal him and let him live. But when God didn't, I didn't carry the guilt that I could have spared his life had I had enough faith. Why? Because I knew the whole counsel of God on the subject. That is what is important, my friend—not just to proof-text some doctrine, but to study it thoroughly and get the whole truth.

My heart rejoices over your diligence in this study. Persevere, my friend.

Notes

Does all this seem heavy to you? Bless your heart! Hang in there! It is vital that you know the whole counsel of God. Paul realized this truth and thus wrote: "For I have not shunned to declare unto you all the counsel of God. Take heed therefore unto yourselves, and to all the flock, over the which the Holy Ghost hath made you overseers, to feed the church of God, which he hath purchased with his own blood. For I know this, that after my departing shall grievous wolves enter in among you, not sparing the flock. Also of your own selves shall men arise, speaking perverse things, to draw away disciples after them" (Acts 20:27–30 KJV).

If you do not know the whole counsel of God on prayer, you can be led astray. People flock to this "faith" message, grab hold of it without searching the Scriptures carefully to see if it is true, then run half-cocked with it, and end up doing untold harm. Not only do they teach wrong doctrine based on experience, but many times their own faith is eventually devastated when the teaching they have proclaimed to others does not work in their time of need. Enough. Carefully read 1 John 5:14–15 and John 15:7 as printed out for you. When you finish, answer the questions that follow.

> And this is the confidence which we have before Him, that, if we ask anything according to His will, He hears us. And if we know that He hears us in

whatever we ask, we know that we have the requests which we have asked from Him (1 John 5:14–15).

"If you abide in Me, and My words abide in you, ask whatever you wish, and it shall be done for you" (John 15:7).

1. According to 1 John 5:14–15, what is the condition for prayer that will be heard and answered by God?

2. If I fulfill these conditions, what do I have before God in prayer? (I am looking for a word from the text.)

3. According to both these passages, when can I be assured that God will give me what I have asked for?

4. Do you see any connection in the conditions for an answered prayer in these two passages? If so, explain. If not, explain.

5. If you combine these Scriptures with those from yesterday as a composite of teaching, what precepts

will you have on prayer? Make a list of what these Scriptures teach regarding effective prayer. Press on to maturity! Do your homework!

Notes

I think by now you have seen that if you expect God to answer your prayers, you must ask in accordance with His will. "If we ask anything according to His will, He hears us" (1 John 5:14). Then the question becomes, "How do I know His will?" Good question, isn't it?

John 15:7 has the answer, so hang in there while I try to explain it on paper. "If you abide in Me, and My words abide in you, ask whatever you wish, and it shall be done for you." There's the promise: ask whatever you wish, and it shall be done for you. Yet with that promise there is a condition! The condition is that you are to abide in Him and His words are to abide in you. This condition is the key to knowing the will of God.

First, if you are to know the will of God, you will have to abide in Him. The word *abide* means "to be at home with, to dwell with." It carries the idea of remaining with or continuing in so as to endure. When you abide with someone, you get to know them.

Let me give you a personal illustration. People are curious about me because they see me on the platform or on television, or they hear my tapes or radio program, yet that is their only contact with me. So when they can, they question those close to me and in a hundred different ways ask, "What is Kay really like?" Inquisitive people have asked our sons, "Does your mother cook?" . . . "Do you ever see her?" Many who hear my Jeremiah-type message cannot imagine me laughing, playing, or just relaxing. In fact, many times when we get silly, the staff will say, "If they could see you now!" Why don't people see the "whole" me? Why do they only know a few aspects of my character? Why? Simply because we do not abide together.

This is why some women once spoke up and said, "If Kay knew that, she would disapprove." Well, they were wrong. I do not disapprove of a church charging seven dollars per person to come and hear me speak at a day-and-a-half conference. Now, bless their hearts, the women who spoke up thought they were right in speaking for me, but they were wrong. They had heard me say that I never charge, and will never charge, for going and sharing God's Word. I personally do not believe it is pleasing to my God for me as a teacher of His Word to do that. However, I did not say people should not be charged for attending a conference. Why, we charge for conferences at Precept Ministries. It costs to house and feed people, to have our staff work so the conference runs smoothly, and to fly in a speaker. That is reality. They had misapplied my words because they took them out of context.

We can misinterpret God in the same way if we do not abide in Him and His words do not abide in us. That is why we must spend time alone with Him, why His Word is to dwell in us richly . . . so we fully know Him and His will and, therefore, do not speak out of turn.

We will talk about this more tomorrow. The question for today is, "How much do you abide in Him and how much do His words abide in you?" Why? Write out your answer so you can deal with it in an objective way.

Notes

"But how do I know what God's will really is?" you ask. "If I have to pray according to His will in order to get my prayers answered, how am I going to learn to discern His will?"

That's it! You hit it with that last question. I believe discerning God's will is a spiritual art learned by sitting at His feet.

Go back to the Lord's Prayer for a minute. Remember it begins with worship of the Father and moves to allegiance and a heart's cry to do His will . . . it's a longing, a willing submission. Did you notice at this point in the Lord's Prayer that no requests have been made? Here, Beloved, is the key. Before you ever ask God for anything, you need to wait before Him, to abide in:

1. His relationship to you . . . as your Father.

2. His sovereignty . . . for He lives in heaven, ruling over all.

3. His holiness . . . His attributes that make Him God.

When you take these things into consideration, submission to His will follows naturally. Do you want your own way if it goes against His best, His purpose, His will for you?

There may be a fleshly struggle. But surely if you will fulfill the first two principles of the Lord's Prayer, your struggle will end in words similar to those of our Lord Jesus when He prayed in Gethsemane saying, "Father, if Thou art willing, remove this cup from

Me; yet not My will, but Thine be done" (Luke 22:42).

He did not want to go through the hell of the cross, for on that cross He would be made a curse for us (2 Corinthians 5:21; Galatians 3:13). Yet He came to do the will of the Father. Oh, Beloved, can't you see that Jesus is our living example of those first two principles in the Lord's Prayer—worship and submission?

As you abide in Him through worship and time in the Word, His words will abide in you. Then, because you know His will, you will be able to ask according to His will.

"But, Kay," you ask, "how can I specifically know His will?" I think the answer is threefold. We will look at the first two factors today.

Romans 12:1–2 says, "I urge you therefore, brethren, by the mercies of God, to present your bodies a living and holy sacrifice, acceptable to God, which is your spiritual service of worship. And do not be conformed to this world, but be transformed by the renewing of your mind, that you may prove what the will of God is, that which is good and acceptable and perfect."

Did you note the phrase, "that you may prove what the will of God is"? You will never know the will of God until first you worship Him as God by presenting your body a living and holy sacrifice, for that "is your spiritual service of worship." Second, you must be "transformed by the renewing of your mind."

What does it mean to "present yourself a living sacrifice"? The two words, *living* and *sacrifice*, don't seem to go together, do they! When we think of biblical sacrifices, we think of something or someone (our Lord) dying.

Jesus died and rose again from the dead that we who were dead in our trespasses and sins might live. This is the Gospel. And that Gospel is exactly what Paul explains in great detail in Romans 1–11. Then when he finishes, in Romans 12:1–2, under the inspiration of the Holy Spirit, he explains how we are to live, how we are to respond to so great a salvation: We who were dead and have been granted life ought now to respond by living for Him, not according to our way, our dictates, our thoughts, our evaluations, or our desires, but in total submission to whatever God wants to do with us or through us. Like Jesus, you and I are to put ourselves on the altar of sacrifice and say, "Not my will, but Thine be done."

Oh, Beloved, stop and think with me for a minute. If each child of God truly did this, think of how much farther the Gospel would go. Think of how much more money there would be for missions, for the work of the Lord. Think of how much more effective our witness would be, for there would be less fear of man and more fear of God, more holy boldness and less compromise in order to save our skin, our reputation, our comfort, and maybe even our lives! Think of how much more arresting our lives would be, captivating the world's curiosity and interest as they see that we so love and trust Jesus that we would live such sacrificial lives. Even as I write this, I am convicted to examine my own life. Am I truly living sacrificially with all on the altar for my God, claiming absolutely nothing as my own?

Think about it. Why must our minds be renewed? Stop and think, Beloved.

How much of what you were taught as you grew up was based on biblical principles? How many of your teachers were children of God, students of and believers in the Word of God? How many of them believed that it is the pure, unadulterated Word of Almighty God, without error and accurate in all it says?

How much of what is seen and heard in the media or read in print directed your thinking toward biblical standards and precepts? What did you absorb, concentrate on, and learn before you came to know the Lord Jesus Christ?

Do your thinking, your reasoning, and your beliefs need adjusting? There's only one way you are going to know, my friend, and that is by getting in the Word and studying it systematically—not a verse here and a verse there, but book by book. As you do this, you will find your mind being renewed as you are confronted with absolute truth. When you come across something in the Bible that is contrary to the way you think, believe, or live, then you have had an encounter with truth and an adjustment is required. When you make that adjustment, you have renewed your mind . . . and the prayer of our Lord is being answered.

Just before Jesus went to the Garden of Gethsemane where He was arrested, He prayed for you. He prayed, "'I do not ask Thee to take them out of the world, but to keep them from the evil *one*. They are not of the world, even as I am not of the world. Sanctify them in the truth; Thy word is truth'" (John 17:15–17).

To sanctify something is to set it apart. And it is knowing, believing, and living the Word of God, Beloved, that sets you apart. Why? Because His Word is truth. Therefore, if what you have believed isn't in agreement with the Word of God, what you have believed is wrong. It's a lie, and your mind needs to be renewed.

Remember, my friend, before you came to know the Lord you were by nature a child of wrath, a son of disobedience. Listen carefully to what God says in Ephesians 2:1–3: "And you were dead in your trespasses and sins, in which you formerly walked according to the course of this world, according to the prince of the power of the air, of the spirit that is now working in the sons of disobedience. Among them we too all formerly lived in the lusts of our flesh, indulging the desires of the flesh and of the mind, and were by nature children of wrath, even as the rest."

Now, think about what Jesus said about the devil. You may know the verse, but don't skip over it. Think about it and the depth of what Jesus is saying: "You are of *your* father the devil, and you want to do the desires of your father. He was a murderer from the beginning, and does not stand in the truth, because there is no truth in him. Whenever he speaks a lie, he speaks from his own *nature*; for he is a liar, and the father of lies" (John 8:44).

The devil is a liar. Yes, sometimes he does inter-weave truth with his lies. He did this when he tempted Jesus, but Jesus was able to sort it all out because He knew the Word of God—the whole counsel of God. And you must, too, beloved child of God. That is why you must renew your mind by saturating it with the whole counsel of God.

This is a lifetime task. It is also a liberating exercise, for "you shall know the truth, and the truth shall make you free" (John 8:32). And, of course, it will help you to pray more effectively because you will then know how to pray according to the Word of God. As a matter of fact, as I have renewed my mind more and more, I find myself praying back the Word of God to God. It is awesome, because when I do, I know that my prayers are biblical. But, remember, you must pray according to the whole counsel of the Word. You can't claim verses out of context.[4]

---

4 If you want to renew your mind, may I suggest that you start with a wonderful series designed to help you do exactly that. It's the *International Inductive Study Series*, published by Harvest House. These are Bible studies that enable you to dig deeper into God's Word in just fifteen minutes a day! Just go to your local Christian bookstore and ask to see the series. Get one book, work through it, and see how God renews your mind! If you want to learn how to study God's Word inductively, write to Precept Ministries, P.O. Box 182218, Chattanooga, Tennessee 37422, and ask for information on our *Precept Upon Precept* and *In & Out* courses. I would also recommend *The International Inductive Study Bible*, a unique study Bible that helps you discover God's truth on your own.

Notes

Yesterday I said there are basically three ways one can know the will of God. The first is through the worship of sacrifice. The second is through knowing the whole counsel of God. God never acts contrary to His Word or His character. He has magnified His Word above His name (Psalm 138:2).

Now we will look at the third way one can know God's will today.

John 15:7 says, "If . . . My words abide in you, ask . . . ." The Greek word for "words" in this context is *rhema*.

Basically there are two Greek words used to refer to the Word of God: *logos* and *rhema*.

The word *logos* denotes "(I) the expression of thought . . . (a) as embodying a conception or idea (b) a saying or statement (c) discourse, speech, of instruction (II) The Personal Word, a title of the Son of God."[5]

Rhema "denotes that which is spoken, what is uttered in speech or writing . . . The significance of *rhema* (as distinct from *logos*) is exemplified in the injunction of take 'the sword of the Spirit, which is the word of God,' Ephesians 6:17; here the reference is not to the whole Bible as such, but to the individual scripture which the spirit brings to our remembrance

5 W. E. Vine, *An Expository Dictionary of New Testament Words* (Nashville, Tennessee: Thomas Nelson Publishers, 1952), 1241.

for use in time of need, a prerequisite being the regular storing of the mind with Scripture."[6]

In light of all this, what is God saying in John 15:7 about the will of God? I believe I can know the will of God in a particular situation when God, by His Spirit, brings to my mind a *rhema*, a specific Scripture for me to apply to a specific situation.

As you wait upon God, worshiping Him, willing to do His will whatever it might be, then God can let you know through a *rhema* what His desire is in a particular situation.

Now does this mean that you must always have a *rhema* from the Lord before you can know God's will? No! No! No! You also can know His will simply by abiding in Him. There are certain things I do not need to ask God about. Why? Because I know His Word, I know Him, and when I bring my questions or my decisions to the light of the knowledge of Him and His Word, I automatically have His answer. I am "filled with the knowledge of His will in all spiritual wisdom and understanding" (Colossians 1:9). That is the beauty of abiding in Him and having His words abide in me—sometimes, simply just because I know His Word, I know His will.

When I speak about a *rhema*, a specific Scripture that the Lord brings to your mind, please don't forget to consider this in the light of all I have said previously. So many people like to tell others that they have had a "rhema" from the Lord and, therefore, the

---

6 Ibid., 1242.

other person needs to do "such and such." But we have to be very careful in this respect. Not all who say they have a "rhema" from the Lord necessarily have a word from the Lord. And just as they will be held accountable before God for what they speak and do, so you and I will be held accountable before the Lord for what we do with what we hear.

What is our safeguard so we will not be led by anything or anyone but God? Well, to live according to Romans 12:1–2 is the beginning. But we also need to spend time simply sitting at the feet of our Lord, listening to Him. Then whatever He tells us, we are to do.

Look up Luke 10:38–42 and read it carefully. Now, list below what you learn from this passage about Martha and about Mary. As you do, also note what instructions and/or promises Jesus gives to each of them.

MARTHA   MARY

Now, Beloved, make sure your "rhemas" are God's *rhemas*. Learn to sit at His feet and listen. Don't be in a hurry. As you give yourself this quiet time before the Lord, you'll hear His voice and know how to pray according to the will of God.

Notes

"But what if you still don't know what the will of the Lord is because the Word is not specific on the issue at hand? Or what if you don't have a *rhema* from the Lord. What do you do then?" you ask.

Then I go to the Lord and say, "Father, I do not know how to pray. This is what I want or think (and then I tell Him what I want or think), but I only want Your will for me (for whomever). Above all else, Father, glorify Yourself."

Now some will say that praying in this way will never work. How can you pray believing when you don't know what the will of God is? For example, even though I don't know whether God wants to physically heal a person or to use his or her illness to glorify Himself, I can still believe in Him and rest in the fact that if I am worshiping Him and am willing to submit to His will no matter what, He will honor my prayer of, "Thy will be done—whatever it is!"

For heaven's sake, Beloved, and I mean *for heaven's sake*, realize that He is your Father. God knows how to raise, to train, and to guide His children. All He needs is a cooperative child. So learn to "trust in the LORD with all your heart, and do not lean on your own understanding. In all your ways acknowledge Him, and He will make your paths straight" (Proverbs 3:5–6).

"But what if I think I know God's will, and I trust, and I wait, and it doesn't come to pass? What do I do then?"

Simply tell God that you missed it, that you heard Him wrong, and go forward. Put your hand back into His. Don't get disillusioned and pout. God didn't fail. You just missed it. Quit crying.

I mentioned my dad earlier. Well, several years ago when he was sick, I thought God told me Daddy would live. I even thought I had a *rhema*. After five major operations in twelve days and about forty days in the hospital, Daddy died. I was wrong about the will of God. What can I do about it? Let it defeat me? Let it make me wonder if I could ever discern God's will? Let it cripple my prayer life or my confidence in my God? Let it immobilize me? No! No! No! I must go forward. My God is greater than all my mistakes. He is a God of hope! My heart is fully His. He knows it. That is all that matters.

Understand? Oh, I pray so!

Now there is one last thing I want to say about knowing God's will, and it is important. Please listen carefully because I do not want you to misunderstand me. Sometimes when seeking God in prayer, we grab a Scripture that relates to our particular situation in one way or another and claim it as God's will. This cannot always be done. For instance, we may take James 5:14–15 and apply it when we want a healing.

> Is anyone among you sick? Let him call for the elders of the church, and let them pray over him, anointing him with oil in the name of the Lord; and the prayer offered in faith will restore the one who is sick, and the Lord will raise him up, and if he has committed sins, they will be forgiven him (James 5:14–15).

However, those verses are not cure-all verses. We can only apply them if the Lord says this is the verse for a particular illness. Note the phrase, "the prayer offered in faith." "In faith" means God has confirmed His will to heal that particular person.

At times I am asked to pray for someone who is sick. When this happens, I always ask our Father, "How should I pray?" Once a missionary was dying of terminal cancer. The Lord laid it on my heart to pray for healing, so my prayer offered in faith was answered!

I felt I had to share this, whether you agree or not, for this is where so many become disillusioned. They claim Scriptures and do not always see the result they expect.

Now do not get me wrong! Certain Scriptures are basic truths or promises, waiting for faith's application. Yet, even Paul was not healed of his thorn because God had a purpose in it (2 Corinthians 12:7).

Think on these things, Beloved, and search His Word carefully.

Notes

Have you ever finished your prayer time and felt it was absolutely useless?

I have. It is *so* frustrating. My emotions after such times have varied from a feeling of total impotence, to guilt (because of a wandering mind), to a sense of despair. I have wondered, "Father, will I ever learn, or am I to remain retarded in prayer for the rest of my days?"

Surely Jesus sensed this would happen to us, for prayer is probably the most disciplined and difficult exercise in the Christian's life. Oh, how I love this God of ours who has truly promised to supply all of our needs . . . even our need in prayer. How I thank Him for opening my eyes to see what Jesus was doing when He said, "Pray, then, in this way."

It has been so exciting to realize that the Lord's Prayer is an index prayer, a collection of brief sentences, each suggesting a subject of prayer. Now we know *how* to pray. All we have to do is recite one sentence of this prayer at a time, realize what topic or point it covers, and then simply talk to the Father about anything that falls under that particular part of the index.

Then when we finish the first point, we move on to the second. To go through the whole collection of index sentences is to cover the whole plane of prayer. Or, as G. Campbell Morgan, the prince of expositors, said, "To pray that prayer intelligently is to have nothing else to pray for. It may be broken up, each

petition may be taken separately and expressed in
other ways, but in itself, it is exclusive and exhaus-
tive."

"Oh, Father, thank You, thank You, thank You for
this instruction from Your Son."

Oh, Beloved, do you see? Memorize the Lord's
Prayer and no one can take away from you God's way
to pray. From the youngest babe in Christ to the most
mature saint, here is the way each can pray and know
that his or her prayers are pleasing to God. It's a form
of prayer that will expand more and more as you
deepen in your knowledge and walk with Him. It is
a way to pray that will grow with you.

"But, Kay," you may say, "where is intercession on
behalf of others? I did not see it in the Lord's Prayer,
and surely God wants us to pray for others!"

Yes, He does! I asked our Father the same question, and He showed me where it was! I got excited!
Let me show you. Go back to Day Four and read the
Lord's Prayer. As you read, mark every singular personal pronoun: *I, me, my, mine.* Then mark the plural
personal pronouns: *we, our.* Also mark every use of *us.*

Now, before you read on, answer the question,
"Where is intercession in the Lord's Prayer?"

When you pray "this way," you are praying for
yourself as well as for us—the body of Jesus Christ.
Therefore, each index sentence is meant to stimulate

not only petition for yourself but also intercession for the body of Jesus Christ.

"But, Kay, where does the lost world come in?" Another good question. It comes in the index, "Thy kingdom come."

Those who pray for the coming of the Kingdom know that they must intercede for lost souls. The Kingdom cannot come until His body is complete, until the last of His sheep is brought into the fold, for He will not lose one of His (John 10, 17). "The Lord is not slow about His promise [to return and set up His Kingdom], as some count slowness, but is patient toward you, not wishing for any to perish but for all to come to repentance" (2 Peter 3:9). Therefore, when you pray for the coming of His Kingdom, you are "hastening the coming of the day of God" (2 Peter 3:12).

Oh, isn't this wonderful! You have a way to pray—an effective way. Pray, Beloved, pray. And when you pray, do not forget the "us." In fact, today why don't you use the Lord's Prayer simply as a means of intercession for others? See how it works! I'll get you started . . . .

Our Father—"Oh, Father, I want to pray for _____ because he (she) cannot call You Father."

Thy will be done—"Oh, Father, I pray for the president of our country. May he seek Your will above all else, desiring it more than the approval of men. Keep him from the counsel of ungodly men."

You take it from here!

Notes

We must move on to our fourth index sentence, "Give us this day our daily bread." Did you note the word "us"? Remember, when we pray we are not praying for ourselves alone, but rather for the whole body of Christ living in every nook and cranny of this world.

This fourth index sentence contains a major principle of prayer. I don't want to tell you what it is because I want you to see it for yourself—if you see it, it will stick better. And I want it to stick! So let me show it to you by giving you parallel Scriptures that contain the same principle.

Read the following Scriptures and circle the key repeated word in each verse.

"And whatever you ask in My name, that will I do, that the Father may be glorified in the Son" (John 14:13).

"Truly, truly, I say to you, if you shall ask the Father for anything, He will give it to you in My name" (John 16:23).

"And I say to you, ask, and it shall be given to you; seek, and you shall find; knock, and it shall be opened to you. For everyone who asks, receives; and he who seeks, finds; and to him who knocks, it shall be opened" (Luke 11:9–10).

"And all things you ask in prayer, believing, you shall receive" (Matthew 21:22).

"You did not choose Me, but I chose you, and appointed you, that you should go and bear fruit, and that your fruit should remain, that whatever you ask of the Father in My name, He may give to you" (John 15:16).

How do these verses parallel with, "Give us this day our daily bread"? Write out your answer.

Finally, look at James 4:1–3:

What is the source of quarrels and conflicts among you? Is not the source your pleasures that wage war in your members? You lust and do not have; so you commit murder. And you are envious and cannot obtain; so you fight and quarrel. You do not have because you do not ask. You ask and do not receive, because you ask with wrong motives, so that you may spend it on your pleasures.

Let's compare this passage in James with Isaiah 31:1:

Woe to those who go down to Egypt for help, and rely on horses, and trust in chariots because they are many, and in horsemen because they are very strong, but they do not look to the Holy One of Israel, nor seek the LORD!

How do these last two Scriptures correlate with the other Scriptures you looked at today and with the fourth index sentence of the Lord's Prayer?

What have you learned that you can apply to your life?

Notes

What did you see yesterday about prayer? Prayer shows your total dependence upon God, for you are to go to Him asking for the supply of your daily needs. Remember what we saw in the early days of this study? We are coming to our Father who is in heaven. "Every good thing bestowed and every perfect gift *is from above, coming down from the Father . . . " (James 1:17, italics added).

Thus, a major precept of prayer is asking. You may not like that. You may feel it is not right. You may think you ought to get what you need on your own. But, Beloved, you are wrong. God has promised to "supply all your needs according to His riches in glory in Christ Jesus" (Philippians 4:19).

To try and have your needs met apart from seeking Him is to end up in a state of internal war, finding yourself riddled with lust and envy, with your pleasures waging war in your members (James 4:1–2). To try to have your needs met apart from trusting in God is to end up in quarrels and conflicts with others (James 4:1). To try to have your needs met independently of Him is to deny your need of Him and His promises (Philippians 4:19). To go to others for help instead of to your Father is to live a life of woe (Isaiah 31:1), to be cursed. For "thus says the LORD, 'Cursed is the man who trusts in mankind and makes flesh his strength, and whose heart turns away from the LORD. For he will be like a bush in the desert and will not see when prosperity comes, but will live in stony wastes in the wilderness, a land of salt without inhabitant" (Jeremiah 17:5–6).

However, those who live in total dependence upon God have this promise: "Blessed is the man who trusts in the LORD and whose trust is the LORD. For he will be like a tree planted by the water, that extends its roots by a stream and will not fear when the heat comes; but its leaves will be green, and it will not be anxious in a year of drought nor cease to yield fruit" (Jeremiah 17:7–8).

Why, oh, why will we not humble ourselves, get rid of our pride, and realize that apart from Him we can do nothing, not even supply our own needs?

"But," you may say, "those who do not know Jesus supply their own needs and they survive!" Yes, they do survive! But how do they survive? Don't they live in constant concern about their material possessions . . . having them or keeping them? They are struggling all the time. They do not realize it is only because of who God is that they have what they have, "for He causes *His* sun to rise on the evil and the good, and sends rain on the righteous and the unrighteous" (Matthew 5:45, italics added). "Who among all these does not know that the hand of the LORD has done this, in whose hand is the life of every living thing, and the breath of all mankind?" (Job 12:9–10).

Oh, can you not see why we need to pray, "Give us this day our daily bread"?

How dependent are you upon God? Do you trust in God or in man?

Notes

"But how do I ask?" you say. "For what do I ask?"

You are to ask for everything—from the basic necessities up! I believe that is why this index sentence mentions "daily bread." Can't you see how this relates to His command, "Pray without ceasing" (1 Thessalonians 5:17)? Since in Him we live and move and have our being, we are to be ever in communion with Him, worshiping, giving allegiance, submitting, seeking His will, asking for our needs, confessing our sins, seeking His protection. All this not only for ourselves—but for others!

When I look at this imperative from God to pray without ceasing, I see it as a command to walk in continual dependence upon Him, realizing that He is a God who is there. He is a God who will supply all my needs, from the need to worship to the need for protection from the evil one. Thus, I am to commune with Him without ceasing as if He were by my side at all times—which He is!

How do I ask? Again, I am to ask according to His will. And how do we come to know the will of God? By abiding in Him and by having His words abide in us.

How then do you ask? By pleading the promises of God. "For as many as may be the promises of God, in Him they are yes . . . " (2 Corinthians 1:20).

D. L. Moody said, "Tarry at a promise and God will meet you there." This wonderful principle of pleading the promises of God was crystallized for me when

I read the following from Armin Gesswein's *School of Prayer:*

Early in the ministry I had an experience which completely changed my understanding of prayer. What a transformation! I was called to start churches and had just discovered "prayer meeting truth" in the Acts. So I started a prayer meeting—the first one I ever attended.

In came an elderly Methodist one night. When he prayed, I detected something new. "I have never heard praying like that," I said to myself. It was not only fervency—I had plenty of that. Heaven and earth got together at once when he prayed. There was a strange immediacy about it. The prayer and the answer were not far apart—in fact they were moving along together. He had it "in the bag" so it seemed to me. The Holy Spirit was right there, in action, giving him assurance of the answer even while he was praying! When I prayed, God was "way out there," somewhere in the distance, listening. The answer, too, was in the distance, in the bye and bye.

Eager to learn his secret, I went to see him one day. His name was Ambrose Whaley, and everyone called him "Uncle Am." He was a retired blacksmith—also a Methodist lay preacher. I soon came to the point, "Uncle Am, I would love to pray with you." At once he arose, led me outside across the driveway into a red barn, up a ladder, into a haymow! There, in some old hay, lay 2 big Bibles—one open. "What is this?" I thought. I prayed first, as I recall it. Poured out my heart, needs, burdens, wishes, aspirations, ambitions to God. Then he prayed—and there was "that difference" again. There, in that hay, on our knees, at the eyeball level, I said: "Uncle Am, what is it? . . . you have some kind of a *secret* in praying. Would you mind sharing it with me?"

I was 24, he was 73 (he lived to be 93), and with an eagle-look in his eyes, he said: "YOUNG MAN, LEARN TO PLEAD THE PROMISES OF GOD!"

That did it! My praying has never been the same since. That word completely changed my understanding of prayer. It really revolutionized it! I "saw it" as soon as he said it. Saw what? Well—when I prayed there was fervency, ambition, etc. (The Lord does not put a "perfect squelch" on these either.) But I lacked FAITH. Prayer is the key to heaven, but faith unlocks the door. THERE MUST BE FAITH. Where does that come from? From hearing . . . the WORD OF GOD. Uncle Am would plead Scripture after Scripture, reminding Him of promise after promise, pleading these like a lawyer does his case— the Holy Spirit pouring in His assurance of being heard. This man knew the promises "by the bushel." He did not seem to need those 2 Bibles in that hay! I soon learned that he was a mighty intercessor. He prayed "clear through." He prayed THROUGH THE BIBLE. He taught me the secret of intercessory praying. How can I ever thank God enough for leading me to such a prayer warrior!

WHAT HAPPENED? With this discovery, God really GAVE ME A NEW BIBLE! I had not yet learned how to make the Bible MY PRAYER BOOK. It gave me a new motivation for Bible study. I began to "dig in!" I would now search the Scriptures . . . meditate . . . mark its many promises . . . memorize, memorize, MEMORIZE! There are thousands of promises: a promise for every need, burden, problem, situation.

"YOUNG MAN, LEARN TO PLEAD THE

PROMISES OF GOD!" These words keep ringing in my soul!

Uncle Am wasn't the only one who pled the promises of God! He had a long line of predecessors.

Search the Old Testament, observe the prayers of those men of God, and you will find them constantly reminding God of His promises to Abraham, Isaac, and Jacob, to His covenant people Israel.

Take a few minutes and look at Moses' prayer in Exodus 32:9–14, then answer the questions that follow.

[9] And the LORD said to Moses, "I have seen this people, and behold, they are an obstinate people. [10] Now then let Me alone, that My anger may burn against them, and that I may destroy them; and I will make of you a great nation." [11] Then Moses entreated the LORD his God, and said, "O LORD, why doth Thine anger burn against Thy people whom Thou hast brought out from the land of Egypt with great power and with a mighty hand? [12] Why should the Egyptians speak, saying, 'With evil intent He brought them out to kill them in the mountains and to destroy them from the face of the earth'? Turn from Thy burning anger and change Thy mind about doing harm to Thy people. [13] Remember Abraham, Isaac, and Israel, Thy servants to whom Thou didst swear by Thyself, and didst say to them, 'I will multiply your descendants as the stars of the heavens, and all this land of which I have spoken I will give to your descendants, and they shall inherit it forever.'" [14] So the LORD changed His mind about the harm which He said He would do to His people.

1. What provokes Moses to prayer?

2. How does Moses approach God in prayer? By that I mean, on what basis does he begin his prayer?

3. What promise does Moses plead? Why do you think he chose this particular promise?

4. What is the end result of Moses' prayer? Why do you think God answered his prayer?

Do you know the promises to plead, Beloved?

Notes

So often when I sit down at a meal, I cannot help but think of my brothers and sisters who are starving. Truly, America is the land of plenty. Because of our abundance we cannot even imagine what it is like to be without, to be unable to satisfy the gnawing pain of an empty stomach.

When we come to this fourth index sentence, "Give us this day our daily bread," we must remember the "us." And while we are praying, seeking God's provision, we need to remember that this index sentence can be a springboard from which we can pray for all the contingencies that go with an adequate supply of daily bread. God tells us that "entreaties and prayers, petitions and thanksgivings, be made on behalf of all men, for kings and all who are in authority, in order that we may lead a tranquil and quiet life in all godliness and dignity" (1 Timothy 2:1–2). When governments are in disarray, it affects the country and the welfare of its people. Therefore, this is a contingency we need to cover when we pray for daily bread.

Often when I get in the shower, I pray for the beloved Christians who are unable to bathe, for those in prisons for the gospel's sake who do not even have water to wash their bodies. Often I remember Galina whose picture I saw in "A Bible for Russia," a newsletter from a non-profit organization serving the persecuted church. At twenty-two, Galina was interned in a Siberian labor camp because she taught young children about Jesus. She received only one bowl of water a week for washing everything—clothes and body. She worked ten hours a day on starvation rations. At night she slept in a thin wooden building, which was little protection when the temperature dropped to minus 40 degrees, Celsius!

I plead God's Word for her, according to Nahum 1:12–13, verses God laid upon my heart for those under government oppression: "This is what the LORD says: 'Although they are unscathed and are numerous, they will be cut down and pass away. Although I have afflicted you, O Judah, I will afflict you no more. Now I will break their yoke from your neck and tear your shackles away'" (NIV).

One more thought on asking. When you pray, you must remember that effective prayer is brought to the Father in the name of Jesus. It is for this reason that I think we are to pray to the Father through the Son rather than to Jesus. Did you notice how often the Scripture says ask "in My name"? What does that mean? Arno C. Gaebelein states it so well:

> In order to pray in His name it is necessary that the person is in Him and identified with Him. The phrase "in the name" as used in the New Testament generally signifies the representation of the person whose name is used, standing in his stead, fulfilling his purposes, manifesting his will and showing forth his life and glory. To pray, therefore, effectually in His name means realizing our standing in Christ, our union with Him, and seeking His glory. The mere use of the name of our Lord in prayer without the spiritual reality of our oneness with Him and deep desire to glorify Him by having His will done in our

lives is unavailing. But knowing Him and bent on doing His will we can pray in His name.[7]

Oh, Beloved, as we pray, as we come to Him in the matchless name of Jesus, let us not fail to pray for Christ's church.

Following is a chart, "Asking According to God's Will: James 4:1–3." If you will fill it out diligently, I know God will use it as you determine how to pray. Bless you.

7 Arno C. Gaebelein, *Gospel of John* (Neptune, New Jersey: Loizeaux Brothers, Inc., 1965), 279.

ASKING ACCORDING TO GOD'S WILL: JAMES 4:1–3

	WHAT I WANT FOR	WHY I WANT IT	CAN I ASK FOR IT IN JESUS' NAME?	WHAT I AM GOING TO ASK FOR
MY CHURCH				
MY FAMILY				
ME				

Notes

The fifth index sentence in the Lord's Prayer has to do with confession and forgiveness: "And forgive us our debts, as we also have forgiven our debtors." That is a loaded index sentence! How I wish we could spend a couple of weeks on it.

As you look at the order of these index sentences, you realize that Jesus must have had a purpose in the way He gave them. Yet, do you wonder why He waited so long to mention the subject of sin and forgiveness? I did, and I meditated upon it.

It seemed to me if I were to confess sin and to seek to forgive my brother before I did anything else in prayer, it might be a superficial cleansing and would probably make forgiveness more difficult—for immediately my focus is on me! However, when I begin in worship, long for His Kingdom, desire His will, and come to Him seeking His provision for my needs, then confession cannot help but follow!

How can I genuinely worship God, tell Him I desire His will, ask Him to supply my needs, and not be smitten with my sin, with my need of His favor in forgiveness? And knowing His forgiveness, how can I withhold the same pardon, the same grace from those who have trespassed against me? I must have His forgiveness, for I have wounded our Father. I must forgive as He has forgiven me, for to fail to do so is to wound the Lamb of Calvary.

There is one thing God cannot do. He cannot overlook sin. He is holy and, therefore, sin must always be dealt with. It cannot be covered. If you want to see the holiness of God, take a long, careful look at Calvary. Who crucified His only begotten Son on Golgotha's hill of shame? Who let Jesus scream, "MY GOD, MY GOD, WHY HAST THOU FORSAKEN ME" (Matthew 27:46)? Who let Him go into hell (Acts 2:27, 31)?

It was the One with eyes too pure to behold iniquity (Psalm 22:1–3; Habakkuk 1:13)!

It was the One not satisfied with the blood of bulls and goats, which could never take away sin (Hebrews 10:4–8).

It was the One who said, "Without shedding of blood there is no forgiveness" (Hebrews 9:22).

It was the One who at Calvary satisfied His holiness when the sinless Lamb of God was slaughtered by the Father . . . the Lamb who takes away the sin of the world (John 1:29). In His holiness "He [God] made Him [Jesus] who knew no sin to be sin on our behalf, that we might become the righteousness of God in Him" (2 Corinthians 5:21).

"But," you may say, "if my sins were forgiven at Calvary, why must I confess them again, asking His forgiveness? Are they not already forgiven?"

Yes, all sin—past, present, and future—was dealt with at Calvary. We have been "sanctified through the offering of the body of Jesus Christ once for all" (Hebrews 10:10).

But although sin was paid for in full at Calvary, sin unconfessed before the throne of God puts a barrier between God and His child. Why? Think about it in

the light of His character, write down your insights,
and we will talk about it tomorrow.

Notes

There is a principle that applies to saved and lost alike regarding forgiveness: God will not forgive those who will not forgive others. You can argue it, debate it, but it is there in black and white to be believed for what it says.

Read Matthew 18:21-35.

[21]Then Peter came and said to Him, "Lord, how often shall my brother sin against me and I forgive him? Up to seven times?" [22]Jesus said to him, "I do not say to you, up to seven times, but up to seventy times seven. [23]For this reason the kingdom of heaven may be compared to a certain king who wished to settle accounts with his slaves. [24]And when he had begun to settle them, there was brought to him one who owed him ten thousand talents. [25]But since he did not have the means to repay, his lord commanded him to be sold, along with his wife and children and all that he had, and repayment to be made. [26]The slave therefore falling down, prostrated himself before him, saying, 'Have patience with me, and I will repay you everything.' [27]And the lord of that slave felt compassion and released him and forgave him the debt. [28]But that slave went out and found one of his fellow slaves who owed him a hundred denarii; and he seized him and began to choke him, saying, 'Pay back what you owe.' [29]So his fellow slave fell down and began to entreat him, saying, 'Have patience with me and I will repay you.' [30]He was unwilling however, but went and threw him in prison until he should pay back what was owed. [31]So when his fellow slaves saw what had happened, they were deeply grieved and came and reported to their lord all that had happened. [32]Then summoning him, his lord said to him, 'You wicked slave, I forgave

you all that debt because you entreated me. [33] Should
you not also have had mercy on your fellow slave, even
as I had mercy on you?' [34]And his lord, moved with
anger, handed him over to the torturers until he should
repay all that was owed him. [35]So shall My heavenly
Father also do to you, if each of you does not forgive
his brother from your heart" (Matthew 18:21-35).

Now then, let's take a look at what God's Word has
to say about sin as it relates to prayer's effectiveness.
Remember the Scripture from James: "The effective
prayer of a righteous man can accomplish much"?
How righteous does that mean? Does it mean merely
declared righteous, or does it mean declared righteous *and* living righteously?

Answer that question by reading the following
verses. Write your conclusions when you finish.

He who turns away his ear from listening to the law,
even his prayer is an abomination (Proverbs 28:9).

He who conceals his transgressions will not prosper,
but he who confesses and forsakes them will find compassion (Proverbs 28:13).

Behold, the LORD's hand is not so short that it cannot
save; neither is His ear so dull that it cannot hear. But
your iniquities have made a separation between you
and your God, and your sins have hidden His face from
you, so that He does not hear (Isaiah 59:1-2).

If I regard wickedness in my heart, the Lord will not
hear (Psalm 66:18).

FOR THE EYES OF THE LORD ARE UPON THE RIGHTEOUS,
AND HIS EARS ATTEND TO THEIR PRAYER, BUT THE FACE OF

THE LORD IS AGAINST THOSE WHO DO EVIL (1 PETER 3:12).

If we confess our sins, He is faithful and righteous to forgive us our sins and to cleanse us from all unrighteousness (1 John 1:9).

Therefore, confess your sins to one another, and pray for one another, so that you may be healed. The effective prayer of a righteous man can accomplish much (James 5:16).

Now, draw some conclusions from these verses. In the space provided, summarize what you have learned regarding sin and prayer.

When Jesus said, "Forgive us our debts," the debts He was talking about were our moral debts, our sins. We owe God absolute righteousness. To sin is to be in debt!

Have you settled your debts through confessing and forsaking them?

God says, "But to this one I will look, to him who is humble and contrite of spirit, and who trembles at My word" (Isaiah 66:2).[8] For a good prayer of confession, meditate on Psalm 51.[9]

Well, Beloved, tomorrow is our last day. I want to commend you on your diligence in persevering. Only those who finish the race can ever qualify for the crown. Bless you. I pray your prayer life will never be the same. May it deepen in its intimacy with our Father.

---

8 If you feel that all is not right between you and your God, you may want to read my booklet entitled *Cleansing and Filling*. In fact, I suggest you do so. God will meet you in your sincerity and desire for holiness. To order this booklet, contact Customer Services, Precept Ministries, P.O Box 182218, Chattanooga, Tennessee, 37422, or call 423-892-6814.

9 Please remember that when David said in Psalm 51:11, "Do not take Thy Holy Spirit from me," he was still under the Old Covenant (John 1:14; Ephesians 1:13-14).

Notes

Notes

The final index sentence of our Lord's Prayer, "And do not lead us into temptation, but deliver us from evil," has been hard for some to understand.

James says, "Let no one say when he is tempted, 'I am being tempted by God'; for God cannot be tempted by evil, and He Himself does not tempt anyone" (James 1:13). On the surface, this index sentence of the Lord's Prayer seems to contradict the strong admonition from James. However, we know that because all Scripture is inspired by God (2 Timothy 3:16), one Scripture cannot deny another Scripture, nor can it state a contradictory truth, for then it would not be truth! Therefore, the question becomes, "Why did Jesus tell us to pray this way if God does not tempt us to do evil? Why this type of prayer?" I want to answer this carefully, but let me warn you that you need to read what I write thoughtfully because it is loaded. It is a lot of truth packed into one day.

Let's take apart the phrase "do not lead us into temptation." Then we'll dig out the answers to the questions. Follow me carefully. Don't get bogged down.

"Lead" in the Greek, is *eisphero*, which means "to bring to." It is an aorist active subjunctive verb. The aorist tense denotes punctiliar action, occurring at one particular time. The active voice indicates that the subject produces the action of the verb. Therefore, it is God who brings or does not bring us into temptation. The subjunctive mood is a mood of probability and expresses an action which may or should happen but which is not necessarily true at present. Therefore, the statement, "do not lead us into temptation," is saying, in essence, "God, I am asking You not to bring us into temptation at any point in time."

Hang in there! The good part is coming. You're growing. Can't you tell by your growing pains? Now, let's look at temptation. Then we will put it together in a practical way.

The Greek word for "temptation" is *peirasmos* and is used for trials of varied character: trials, testings, temptations. Thus, the word *peirasmos* must be interpreted according to its context. For instance, in James 1:2, 12 *peirasmos* describes a trial we are to rejoice in, while in James 1:13–14 the same root word is used in connection with sin and, therefore, a temptation to be avoided.

What then is Matthew 6:13 saying? Well, we know it is not saying, "God, don't lead me into sin," because that is contrary to the character of God. And it contradicts James 1:13, "Let no one say when he is tempted, 'I am being tempted by God'; for God cannot be tempted by evil, and He Himself does not tempt anyone."

What then is Jesus calling us to cover in prayer? I believe that this index sentence is a reminder or a call to vigilance in "preventive" prayer. When you come to this final topic of prayer, you are letting God know that your heart is set on righteousness, that you do not want to fail, to fall. When you find yourself in a trial (*peirasmos*), if you do not do as James 1:2 says and count it all joy, you are often tempted to give way to your flesh. If you do not realize that "the testing of your faith produces endurance" and you do not "let endurance have its perfect result, that you may be perfect and complete, lacking in nothing" (James 1:3–4), then you are liable to respond improperly in that trial, fall prey to the seducer, and yield to temptation.

Let me give you an illustration. I am writing this while Jack drives, since we had to go to Atlanta for an appointment today. Our appointment was set for 12:30 P.M.; therefore, we had to leave Chattanooga by 10:30 A.M. At 10:25 Jack walked out the door to go to the office. Panicking, I ran after him to tell him we had to leave in five minutes. At 10:35 I poured a cup of coffee for my sweet husband. At 10:45 I called the office in desperation, only to find that my not-so-sweet husband had gone to the bank. To put it bluntly, I was flat-out mad. By 11:00 I was so angry I could have cried. I had so carefully planned my morning for an on-time getaway, and now my plans were going up in smoke. Mine! I sat down to try to read a book on prayer, but concentration was impossible. At 11:05 I heard a horn honk. As I walked out of the door, mouth firmly set in displeasure, James 1:2–3 came to my mind: "Count it all joy . . . temptations . . . worketh patience." I got in the car, started to be ugly, but decided instead to walk in obedience. Our trip was sweet because Kay was obedient . . . but in her flesh she did not want to be. In my trial, if I had not responded properly when I saw Jack, then I would have fallen prey to temptation, let my anger control me, and sinned!

Now, can you begin to see how this index sentence on deliverance works? "Do not lead us into temptation, but deliver us from evil." We are telling God we do not want to be caught in the devil's snare. This is preventive prayer, and it is heard by the Father. Who do you think brought that Scripture to my mind as I walked out the door?

Let me give you another outstanding passage that parallels this index sentence on deliverance. Read Matthew 26:36–44 and then answer the questions that follow. Make sure you do not read any further until you answer all of the questions—don't miss the joy of seeing truth for yourself!

36Then Jesus came with them to a place called Gethsemane, and said to His disciples, "Sit here while I go over there and pray." 37And He took with Him Peter and the two sons of Zebedee, and began to be grieved and distressed. 38Then He said to them, "My soul is deeply grieved, to the point of death; remain here and keep watch with Me." 39And He went a little beyond them, and fell on His face and prayed, saying, "My Father, if it is possible, let this cup pass from Me; yet not as I will, but as Thou wilt." 40And He came to the disciples and found them sleeping, and said to Peter, "So, you men could not keep watch with Me for one hour? 41Keep watching and praying, that you may not enter into temptation [*peirasmos*]; the spirit is willing, but the flesh is weak." 42He went away again a second time and prayed, saying, "My Father, if this cannot pass away unless I drink it, Thy will be done." [43]And again He came and found them sleeping, for their eyes were heavy. [44]And He left them again, and went away and prayed a third time, saying the same thing once more (Matthew 26:36–44).

1. What is the cup Jesus wants His Father to remove? Compare this with John 18:11.

2. How many times does Jesus ask God to remove it?

3. When Jesus asks God to remove the cup, what is His prayer?

4. Do you see any parallel(s) between this prayer and the Lord's Prayer? Write out whatever you see.

5. What is Jesus' instruction during this time to the disciples and Peter?

6. Can you see any parallel(s) between Jesus' instruction in Matthew 26:41 and the index sentence on deliverance in the Lord's Prayer? If so, note them below.

To me, Matthew 26:41, "Keep watching and praying, that you may not enter into temptation," is almost an exact reiteration of what we are to pray in the Lord's Prayer. It is an acknowledgment that our flesh is weak, even though our spirit is willing. It is an awareness of our utter dependence upon our God and our utter impotence against temptation apart from Him. And what happened to Peter? He slept. He did not watch and pray! He denied Jesus because he was not aware that his adversary, the devil, was prowling about as a roaring lion seeking someone to devour (1 Peter 5:8).

This petition for deliverance is an acknowledgment of the reality of war. Aware that Satan desires to sift us as wheat, even as he did Peter (Luke 22:31), we are telling God that we realize we cannot handle him alone. We are willing to stand in righteousness, but God must do the delivering. Oh, how we need to see this truth! Jesus will not have us pray a prayer that God will not answer! Therefore, deliverance is *always* available for those who truly want it. No Christian can ever say, "The devil made me do it!"

We have the promises of 1 Corinthians 10:13: "No temptation has overtaken you but such as is common to man; and God is faithful, who will not allow you to be tempted beyond what you are able, but with the temptation will provide the way of escape also, that you may be able to endure it."

Our final prayer is a prayer for deliverance. It is a cry to God out of poverty of spirit (Matthew 5:3), out of grief for falling short of His standard of holiness (Matthew 5:4), out of meekness (Matthew 5:5), out of a hunger and thirst for righteousness (Matthew 5:6), and out of purity of heart (Matthew 5:8). It is a cry that in its praying says, "Spare me, O Father, from needless trials or testings in which I might find myself tempted." It is a cry of awareness that acknowledges the reality of the evil one and of the Christian's warfare. It is an acknowledgment that the flesh is weak. It is heeding our Lord's admonition to "keep watching and praying, that you may not enter into temptation; the spirit is willing, but the flesh is weak" (Matthew 26:41).

To pray this way, Beloved, is to pray our way to victory, for this prayer says, "I know *we*—my brothers and sisters and I—are in a warfare, and we want to, we will to, we choose to win." Surely those who pray this way are "on the alert with all perseverance and petition for all the saints" and for themselves (Ephesians 6:18).

Although the last sentence, "For Thine is the kingdom, and the power and the glory, forever. Amen," is not in the earliest manuscripts, is it any wonder that it was added as a hallelujah of triumph, of worship? It makes the seventh index sentence, and seven is the number of perfection.

Oh, Beloved, pause a minute. Hush! Listen! Can you not hear the hallelujahs from heaven? Thanks be to God who always causes us to triumph in Christ Jesus (2 Corinthians 2:14)! Here we have the perfect way to pray, taught to us by the One who ever lives to make intercession for the children of God.

So, Beloved, we know how to pray! We know what to pray! Now we need to pray . . . and when you pray . . .

"Pray, then, in this way:
  'Our Father who art in heaven,
    Hallowed be Thy name.
  'Thy kingdom come.
    Thy will be done,
    On earth as it is in heaven

'Give us this day our daily bread.

'And forgive us our debts, as we also have forgiven
  our debtors.

'And do not lead us into temptation, but deliver us
  from evil.

[For Thine is the kingdom, and the power, and
the glory, forever. Amen]'" (Matthew 6:9–13).

Notes

Questions for Group Discussion

First Week: DAY 1 Through DAY 7

In the first week of discussion it will be important for you to establish an atmosphere of congeniality and openness so that people will feel the freedom to share without timidity or embarrassment. And how can you achieve this atmosphere? Bathe this time in prayer, seeking God's presence and guidance. Also, be vulnerable before each other. None of us are experts on prayer, so purpose in your hearts to learn together.

Do not limit yourself to these discussion questions nor seek to follow them rigidly. Rather, use them as a springboard for discussion. Once the discussion gets going, you will be on your way.

In this first session together:

1. Explain why Jesus gives His disciples the Lord's Prayer. What provokes it?

2. What is the Lord's Prayer?

3. What is an index sentence?

4. What topics does the Lord's Prayer cover?

5. Read Hebrews 11:6. What principles do you learn from this verse that apply to prayer?

6. What did you learn from your study on Elijah in James 5? Did God speak to you personally in any special way?

7. Discuss Jehoshaphat's prayer using the questions from Day Six as a guide. How many topics from the Lord's Prayer are covered in Jehoshaphat's prayer?

8. Discuss the names of God and how they can be implemented in worship.

9. What does it mean to hallow God's name?

10. What insights into prayer did you gain through your study this week?

11. What effect, if any, did these insights have on your prayer life?

Close in Prayer

Apply what you have learned this week. So people will not be intimidated, limit prayers to one to three sentences at a time. It would be good to move through the Lord's Prayer topic by topic. Cover the first topic in prayer; then, when there is an adequate pause, move to the second index sentence. Do not be concerned if you feel awkward; that is to be expected. The awkwardness will disappear with time and practice.

Second Week: DAY 8 Through DAY 14

1. Begin by saying the Lord's Prayer sentence by sentence. At the end of each sentence, have one of the group share what topic each sentence covers.

2. What did you learn from Isaiah 36–37 on prayer? Use the questions on Day Eight as a springboard for your discussion.

3. How does Jeremiah worship God in his prayer in Jeremiah 32:16–25?

4. How does Daniel worship God in his prayers in Daniel 2:19–23 and Daniel 9:3–19?

5. Do you have any questions on the fact that prayer is only for those who are truly children of God? If so, go over the Scriptures that were used on Days Nine and Ten.

6. What insights did you glean from the second index sentence, "Thy kingdom come"?

7. What insights did you glean on the importance of the will of God in prayer?

Close in Prayer

Spend your time in prayer this week meditating on the names of God and the characteristics that His names reveal. Hallow His name in prayer.

Third Week: DAY 15 Through DAY 21

1. What did you learn about prayer from 1 John 5:14–15 and John 15:7?

2. Define the word "abide" as it is used in John 15:7. What do you think it means to have His Word abide in you? How would this affect your praying?

3. What is the difference between *rhēma* and *logos*?

4. How can you come to know the will of God? What various ways were mentioned in the lessons?

5. When you go to prayer and do not know the will of God, are you still to pray? How?

6. How do Matthew 21:18–22 and Mark 11:23–24 fit with what you have learned about prayer and submission to the will of God?

7. What is the problem with "believe, confess, and it's yours" type praying in the light of what you studied this week?

8. What did you think about the letter that was shared on Day Fifteen?

9. How can you use the Lord's Prayer in intercession for others?

Close in Prayer

Spend your time in prayer interceding for others, applying what you learned this week.

Fourth Week: DAY 22 Through DAY 28

1. Begin by reviewing the topics of the seven index sentences of the Lord's Prayer.

2. What did you learn about the fourth index sentence?

a. How important is asking?

b. Why do you think God wants us to ask when He knows our needs anyway?

c. Has God ever given you something you asked for in prayer? What? What effect did it have on you?

d. Are there any qualifications for asking (James 4:1–3; John 14:13; 15:16; 16:23; Matthew 21:22; Luke 11:9–10)? Note the present tense of the verb "ask."

3. What does it mean to "plead the promises"? What are some promises we can plead in prayer?

4. What did you learn from Moses' prayer in Exodus 32:9–14? Refer to the questions on Day Twenty-four if necessary.

5. Did the chart on asking help at all? What insights did you gain from filling it out?

6. How does sin keep you from being heard by God? Meditate on the following Scriptures: Proverbs 28:9, 13; Isaiah 59:1–2; Psalm 66:18; 1 Peter 3:12; 1 John 1:9; and James 5:16.

7. What did you learn about confession from Psalm 51?

8. Why is forgiving others pertinent to prayer? You may want to read and meditate on Matthew 18:21–35.

9. Finally, reflect on the meaning of the sixth index sentence—for deliverance.

    a. What problems did you have with this index sentence?

    b. How did you resolve them?

    c. What did Jesus mean when He told us to pray, "Lead us not into temptation"?

    d. How does this index sentence relate to 1 Corinthians 10:13 and Matthew 26:41?

    e. What effect does this prayer have on your conduct as a Christian? How and why?

    10. How has this study affected your prayer life?

Close in Prayer

Pray through the Lord's Prayer topic by topic, closing with the seventh index sentence.

**May our Father richly bless
these discussions and use them to enrich
your communion with Him
and with one another.**

Yes, I want to grow spiritually.
Tell me more about

PRECEPT MINISTRIES INTERNATIONAL

Name _____

Address _____

City _____

State _____ Postal Code _____

Country _____

Daytime phone ( ) _____

Email address _____

Fax ( ) _____

Evening phone ( ) _____

PLEASE SEND ME INFO ON:

❏ Learning how to study the Bible

❏ Bible study material

❏ Radio Programs

❏ TV Programs

❏ Israel Bible Study Tour

❏ Paul's Epistles Study Tour to Greece

❏ Men's Conferences

❏ Women's Conferences

❏ Teen Conferences

❏ Couples' Conferences

❏ Other_____

❏ I want to partner with Precept Ministries
  ENCLOSED IS MY DONATION FOR $_____

P.O. Box 182218 • Chattanooga, TN 37422-7218
(800) 763-8280 • (423) 892-6814 • Radio/TV (800) 763-1990
Fax: (423) 894-2449 • www.precept.org • Email: info@precept.org